Chloë

Tells You How...
To Sew

This book belongs to

....

....

Chloë

Tells You How...
To Sew

More than 30 Things to Make, Do, and Sew

CHLOË OWENS

CICO BOOKS

LONDON NEW YORK

Modern-day hippie chick Chloë Owens spends her time cutting up psychedelic vintage fabrics and stitching them together to make colorful textile "paintings", toys, and home accessories. In this book she has combined her love of 1960s children's comics with her enthusiasm for all things stitched, creating a new kind of craft book that will be loved by people of all ages. She lives in London with her boyfriend D-fran, cat Twiggy, and puppy Ringo.

For D-fran

Published in 2014 by CICO Books
An imprint of Ryland Peters & Small Ltd

20–21 Jockey's Fields 519 Broadway, 5th Floor
London WC1R 4BW New York, NY 10012

www.rylandpeters.com

10 9 8 7 6 5 4 3 2 1

Text © Chloë Owens 2014
Design and photography © CICO Books 2014, except image on p. 2, taken by Claire Richardson for *Mollie Makes* magazine, www.molliemakes.com

A CIP catalog record for this book is available from the Library of Congress and the British Library.

ISBN: 978 1 78249 047 0

Printed in China

Editor: Sarah Hoggett
Designer: Christian Owens
Creative consultant: Chloë Owens
Cover design: Chloë Owens, Claudia Channing
Photographer: Claire Richardson
Illustrators: Ingela Aarhenius, Alice Burrows, Gemma Correll, Nicholas J. Frith, Tom Frost, Tove Larris, Luciano Lozano, Sarah McNeil, and Alice Potter

For digital editions, visit www.cicobooks.com/apps.php

Contents

Hello, pleased to meet you. Come in and sit down. Cup of tea?

My name is Chloë. Welcome to my bumper book of crafts! You've decided to pick it up and open it… maybe you were drawn to it out of nostalgia? Perhaps you're a grown-up who used to collect comic books, or a child who loves to make things? I adored poring over old comic-book annuals as a child, and I decided to combine my crafty know-how with a love of storytelling and puzzles to create a bumper book of projects that will provide hours of fun for all the family.

This is a craft book with a tongue-in-cheek twist. I will teach you how to make things using fabric, appliqué, and stitch. I'd like to inspire you to be creative and really enjoy yourself while you're doing it. A lot of the projects are designed to celebrate fabric. Some are as easy as pie, but will look decidedly beautiful when they're complete. Other projects are a bit more advanced, but just jump right in. The odd wobbly line will just add to the homemade charm and that's what we're aiming for, after all!

I grew up reading my older siblings' hand-me-down comic book annuals from the 1960s and '70s. I would spend hours absorbed in their gripping stories, crafty makes, and amusing games, and soon began collecting vintage annuals from charity shops (thrift stores) to feed my addiction. My favorites were *Diana*, *Playhour*, *Girl*, *Jackie*, and *The Dandy*.

I really liked getting to know the characters as I progressed through the books, meeting them time and again in different stories until they became like old friends. So I dreamed up some "friends" of my own to guide you through my book: meet Doris, who's got a tickety-boo idea for keeping breakfast warm, and Thrifty Thelma and Woolly the lamb, who bring unloved items back to life. All interpreted by some of my favorite illustrators.

For those of you who claim not to be creative… well, that just isn't so! I bet you used to draw and make things as a child. All children love to create. We never lose the joy we found in making things, we just get out of the habit. Take a leap of faith, try one of the projects in this book, and prove yourself wrong!

I loved the fun pages in annuals, too. Coloring in, spot the difference, snakes and ladders… they brought many hours of entertainment and creativity to my childhood, and now bring sentimental and humorous pleasure to my adulthood. So I've included some activities in my book to inject some fun and frolics along the way.

Reading old copies of *Girl*, with its instructions on making beds and tips for filling scrapbooks, are precious echoes of a gentler age. I wanted to create something that commemorated these books, something that makes magical childhood memories come flooding back for grown-ups and inspires modern children with a love of life's simpler pleasures.

So switch off that phone, make yourself cozy, and come with me on a crafting adventure. Who knows where we'll end up?

Chloë's tips

- The projects featured in this book are just a guide for you to work from and for you to add your own personal twists to.

- You can use a freehand machine embroidery foot for a lot of the projects in this book, like me. But if you're partial to hand sewing, then that's fine too!

- I like to stitch in a scribbly, sketchy way, but if you prefer neat or even more scribbly, then you must adapt the designs to suit your preferences.

- I use a lot of vintage fabrics in my work which I get from thrift stores and vintage fairs. I also use new fabrics from some of my favorite fabric designers. You can find their details at the back of this book.

- Felt is a great fabric for beginners to use, because it doesn't fray. Did you know you can buy felt made from recycled plastic bottles? Details at the back of this book!

- You can use fabric scraps cut into small pieces for stuffing.

- Instead of pinning, you can also baste (tack) with a needle and thread. Do whatever you feel most comfortable with.

- Before and during projects, press all fabrics (except felt) so that they're nice and crisp and easy to work with.

- I use a Bernina sewing machine for all my projects; I find it best for freehand machine embroidery.

Please have fun: practice makes perfect!

Throughout this book there are a few fundamental "ingredients" that will be needed for almost all projects. For each project I will then give you another list, which should be added on top of this essential kit.

- Sewing machine
- Freehand machine embroidery foot
- Tape measure
- Pins and needles
- Thread
- Pencil or vanishing fabric marker pen
- Iron and ironing board
- Fabric scissors
- Fabric glue
- Unpicker (for crafty mistakes)

Chloë

TELLS YOU HOW...

... to make a child's pinafore dress

Materials you will need

- TEMPLATES ON PAGES 140–42
- OUTER FABRIC
- LINING FABRIC
- EMBROIDERY FLOSS (THREAD)-OPTIONAL
- TWO BUTTONSS

1 *BEGIN BY MEASURING THE CHILD YOU ARE MAKING THE DRESS FOR AND ADJUST THE TEMPLATES IF NECESSARY. MEASURE ACROSS THE SHOULDERS AND FROM THE NAPE OF THE NECK DOWN TO WHERE YOU WANT THE HEM TO END.*

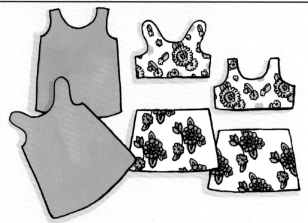

2 *CUT OUT ALL THE PIECES. YOU WILL NEED TWO LINING PIECES, A FRONT AND A BACK TOP, AND A FRONT AND A BACK SKIRT. THEN PRESS THE FABRIC SO THAT IT'S NICE AND CRISP.*

3 *WITH RIGHT SIDES TOGETHER, PIN THE TOPS TO THE CORRESPONDING SKIRT PIECES AND STITCH, TAKING A 3/8-IN. (1-CM) SEAM. PRESS THE SEAMS OPEN.*

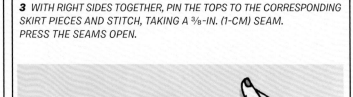

4 *NEXT, WITH RIGHT SIDES TOGETHER, PIN THE FRONT AND BACK PIECES TO THE CORRESPONDING LINING PIECES FROM ARM OPENING TO ARM OPENING. STITCH, TAKING A 3/8-IN. (1-CM) SEAM. TRIM THE SEAM ALLOWANCES, CLIP THE CORNERS, AND NOTCH THE CURVES.*

5 TURN EACH PIECE RIGHT SIDE OUT AND PRESS. LAY THE FRONT AND BACK PIECES RIGHT SIDES TOGETHER. FOLD THE LINING PIECES OUT OF THE WAY, AND PIN THE OUTER DRESSES TOGETHER FROM THE ARM OPENING DOWN TO THE BOTTOM OF THE SKIRT. SEW DOWN BOTH SIDES WITH A ZIG-ZAG STITCH.

6 NEXT, FOLD UP THE OUTER DRESS HEMS TWICE, PIN IN PLACE, AND SEW WITH A STRAIGHT STITCH. REPEAT STEPS 5 AND 6 WITH THE LINING FABRIC.

7 TURN THE DRESS RIGHT SIDE OUT AND GIVE IT A GOOD PRESS.

8 IF YOU WISH, SEW A LITTLE LOOP STITCH WITH EMBROIDERY FLOSS (THREAD) TO JOIN UP THE INNER AND OUTER SEAMS. DO THIS ABOUT 2 IN. (5 CM) UP FROM THE BOTTOM OF THE LINING HEM ON BOTH SIDES; THIS WILL KEEP THEM NEATLY ALIGNED.

9 WITH MATCHING THREAD, TOPSTITCH THE TOP SECTION OF THE DRESS FROM ARMHOLE TO ARMHOLE, FRONT AND BACK, ABOUT ¼ IN. (6 MM) FROM THE EDGE.

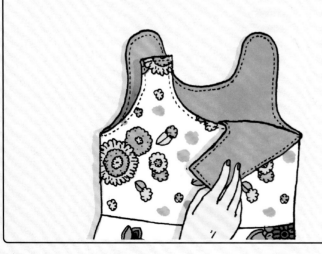

10 TO FINISH THE DRESS, STITCH A BUTTONHOLE ON EACH BACK STRAP (SEE PAGE 112) AND A BUTTON TO EACH FRONT STRAP.

Best seat in the house

Thrifty Thelma and Woolly the Lamb upcycle a chair

Materials you will need

- Old chair with removable cushioned seat
- Screwdriver
- Medium-grit sandpaper
- Damp cloth
- Wood primer paint
- Oil-based paint
- Paintbrush
- Three different upholstery fabrics
- Pliers
- Upholstery or cotton batting (wadding)
- Linen fabric
- Staple gun

1 Thelma and Woolly the Lamb have found an old chair that looks like it has seen better days—one with a removable cushioned seat. Maybe you have one at home? If not, you can find them in thrift stores or charity shops, at vintage fairs, or on sites like eBay.

2 First, they remove the seat using a screwdriver. Woolly puts the screws somewhere safe and they put the seat to one side. They put an old sheet under the chair to protect the floor, and then sand down the wood with medium-grit sandpaper to prepare it for painting. After sanding, Woolly wipes the chair down with a damp cloth so that it's nice and clean.

3 Next, they paint the chair with one coat of wood primer and leave it to dry. Then they paint a thin layer of oil-based paint over the chair, getting it into all the nooks and crannies. Thelma tells Woolly not to paint it on too thickly or it will dry with drips and will easily chip when dry. It will need three coats in total, and they'll need to leave it to dry for 16 hours between each coat.

4 While the paint is drying, Thelma and Woolly get on with the chair seat. They measure the seat and divide the width by three. They use these measurements to cut three pieces of fabric, adding 4 in. (10 cm) to the outside edges of each piece. To each of the inside edges, they add a $^3/_8$-in. (1-cm) seam allowance. You might find it easier to trace around the seat and use paper templates.

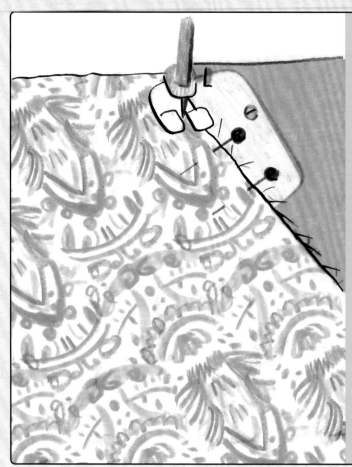

5 They pin the left-hand and middle strip of fabric together along the straight edge. (Thelma explains to Woolly that they need to do this with the right sides of the fabric facing each other or they won't see the pretty fabric when it's all finished.) They sew along the pinned edge, remove the pins, and press the seam open. Then they repeat with the right-hand strip and put the cover to one side.

6 Using a screwdriver and pliers, they remove the staples from the seat and take off the old fabric and batting (wadding).

7 Thelma looks around for some fresh new padding and then has a brilliant idea. She shears Woolly's soft, cushiony fleece "This will work perfectly!" she says. Alternatively, you can find batting (wadding) at your local craft or quilting supplier or from one of the suppliers listed on page 114.

8 Next, Thelma and a not-so-Woolly lay down their stitched cover wrong side up and center the batting (wadding) and chair seat right side down on top. Then they fold the cover over the edges of the seat and staple it in place, folding the corners neatly as they go.

Thelma says...

To make sure the fabric is stretched evenly, pull it taut over the top and bottom edges of the seat, insert one staple in the center of each edge, then repeat on the seat sides. Finally, add extra staples along each edge.

9 Finally, they cut the linen to the size of the seat, lay it on the bottom so that it covers the edges of the stitched cover, fold the raw edges under, and staple all the way around. Then they put the seat back onto the chair and reattach it with the screws they had kept to one side.

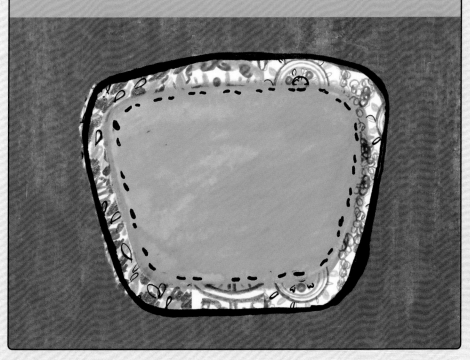

Reversible Collar

Materials you will need

- Templates on page 115
- Two complementary patterned fabrics for the collar
- Felt in colors of your choice
- Ribbon

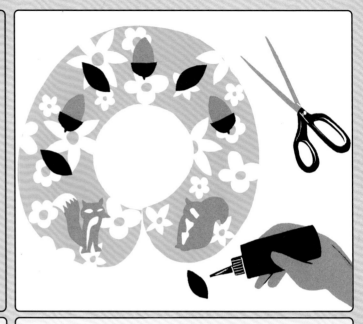

1 First you need to choose two different fabrics for the collar that complement each other well. Cut them out, using the templates on page 115.

2 Now cut out all your pieces for the appliqué design using a variety of felts, and stick them in place on the front piece of your collar using fabric glue.

3 Now to your sewing machine! Lower the feed dogs and, using black thread (or a color of your choice), sew around the felt pieces using a freehand machine embroidery foot.

4 Choose a ribbon, and cut two pieces 12 in. (30 cm) long. Then position them at the curved corners on the collar, so that a little is poking over the edge of the fabric.

Frederick the Fox and Cyril the Squirrel show you how to make a reversible collar

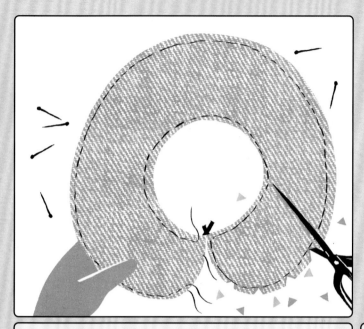

Try making more designs using different fabrics... Every outfit needs a collar.

5 Pin the front and back pieces right sides together, making sure that the ribbon is sandwiched in between. Using a straight stitch and taking a $^3/_8$-in. (1-cm) seam allowance, sew all around the collar, leaving a 2-in. (5-cm) gap for turning. Remove the pins, then notch the curves.

6 Turn the collar right side out and slipstitch the opening closed. Press, and there you have it.

We think you'll look just dandy!

The breeding

1

It was a Saturday in 1964,
And a girl called Mildred was feeling bored.
See, Mildred didn't have many friends,
A lot of time alone she'd spend.

2

She looked at the curtains and blankets on the bed,
She took some scissors and cut them to shreds.
She found some stuffing and collected some threads.
The thought of Mum seeing this filled her with dread.

3

She worked until her hands were scuffed,
Out of breath she felt, and puffed,
She trimmed and embroidered, stitched and stuffed,
She added ears and tails that fluffed.

4

She stitched eyes and noses onto these friends,
She filled them with stuffing through their tail ends.
When she saw what she'd made, she laughed - it was funny!
Around Mildred's bedroom sat 35 bunnies.

5

A sea of rabbits made from satin and felt,
With buttons for eyes and bright fabric for pelt.
She slept well that night, though she was rather chilly...
Maybe cutting up her blankets had been slightly silly.

6

As the moon came out from behind a cloud,
A change came over this unusual crowd.
Suddenly their rabbit eyes started to blink,
Their noses wrinkled, their minds began to think.

Bunnies ...

7

Well when rabbits get friendly, it's a forgone conclusion,
They get in a frenzy, a huge bunny fusion.
Temptation was strong to do the deed,
They soon paired up and bred at great speed.

8

Early next morning, Mildred awoke.
What did she see? Was this a joke?
At the sight of a hundred bunnies Mildred gaped,
Maybe she ought to just let them escape?

9

Mildred's heart pounded and her mouth became dry,
This new infestation made her want to cry.
But as it was Sunday it was time for church,
For her best dress she had to search.

10

Mildred could stand this bizarre sight no more,
She left for church leaving open her door.
The bunnies looked at each other and started to smile,
Out of the doorway they began to pile.

To be continued...

Harvey
the rabbit

Jimmy decides to make a playmate!

Materials you will need

- Templates on pages 120-121
- Blue felt for Harvey's body
- Patterned fabric for Harvey's shirt, pants, inner ear, and bow tie
- Toy filling or fabric scraps
- Black embroidery floss (thread)-optional
- Scrap of pink felt for nose
- Two buttons for eyes
- Three buttons for shirt

Jimmy says...

Cut two arms and legs, then flip the pattern over and cut two more of each!

1 First, Jimmy makes paper patterns from the templates on pages 120-121. Then he finds some felt and fabric and cuts out shapes for all the body pieces and clothes. Now he's ready to start making his new friend!

2 He pins the four felt hand pieces to the right side of the four fabric arm pieces and sews along the straight edge, ⅜ in. (1 cm) from the edge. Then he takes out the pins and presses the seams flat.

3 Next, he pins the arms right sides together and sews all the way around, leaving the top of the arm open. When he's done this, he turns the arms right side out. This can be a bit fiddly, but Jimmy has found a good trick: he uses an unsharpened pencil to poke the closed end into itself, then carefully pushes it along until he can grab the end and pull it through gently.

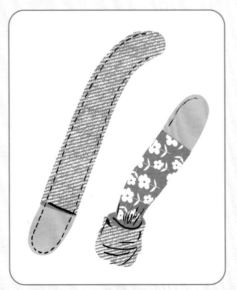

4 He repeats steps 2 and 3 to make the legs. Then he presses the arms and legs and stuffs them firmly, pushing in a little toy filling at a time with a pencil—but not too tightly, otherwise the seams may rip! He pinches and squishes them into shape.

5 Next Jimmy pins the felt and fabric ear pieces right sides together and sews all the way around, leaving the bottom edge open. He doesn't press the ears after stitching, because he wants them to stay nice and plump. For the right ear, he folds the bottom left corner over to two-thirds of the way along the bottom edge, then he folds the bottom right corner in so that it meets the left corner. For the left ear, he does the opposite. He pins and stitches the folds in place using matching thread.

6 Using a vanishing fabric marker pen, Jimmy lightly draws the eyes, whiskers, and mouth on one head piece, then he embroiders these features—you can do this by hand in backstitch using embroidery floss (thread), or use a sewing machine. He cuts a tiny heart shape from pink felt for the nose and glues it in place, then he sews on two green buttons for eyes.

7 With right sides together, Jimmy pins the embroidered head to the top of the rabbit's shirt, and stitches them together, ⅜ in. (1 cm) from the edge. Then he pins the top of the pants to the bottom of the rabbit's shirt, right sides together again, and stitches them together. He does the same for the back pieces and presses all the seams open. He sews three buttons to the front of the rabbit's shirt.

8 Jimmy makes the rabbit a bow tie (see pages 84-5) and hand stitches it just below the seam beneath the rabbit's head.

9 Time for a rabbit "sandwich!" Jimmy lays the front of the rabbit right side up and places the ears, arms, and legs in position, with the open ends poking slightly over the edges. Then he lays the back of the rabbit on top, right side down this time, and pins everything firmly into place.

10 He sews all the way around his rabbit sandwich, leaving a 4-in. (10-cm) opening at the side. He turns the rabbit right side out and stuffs him with toy filling. Then he sews up the opening by hand using a slipstitch.

Jimmy calls him Harvey and they become very good friends.

Funny face egg warmers

Doris makes some tickety-boo cozies

Materials you will need

- Templates on pages 135–37
- Tracing paper, pencil, and cardstock
- Red, white, and pink felt
- Black and blue embroidery flosses (threads)
- Scraps of fabric for the bow

1 One morning Doris is eating her eggs and "facon" (fake bacon—if you don't know Doris, she's a strict vegetarian). But as she tucks in, she is most perturbed to find that her eggs have already gone cold! "Oh bother!" she cries. "What is a girl to do?"

2 She ponders for a while as she finishes her breakfast, and suddenly a spiffing idea pops into her head! She gathers some felts and collects her sewing materials, and draws the shapes she will need.

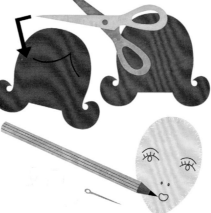

3 First, Doris makes cardstock templates for the hair and face shapes she has drawn (you can use the ones on pages 135–37).

4 She draws around the hair template twice on red felt and cuts out two hair shapes. Using sharp scissors, she cuts a curved V-shape slit in one hair shape to make a fringe. Then she cuts two faces from white felt in the same way, pins them together, and blanket stitches (see page 113) all the way around with matching thread. Using a pencil, she draws the features on one side of the face.

Why not make a smiley-faced egg cozy for each member of your family? You can change the hair color and hairstyle, add a moustache or beard for the boys, or even make them look like people you know!

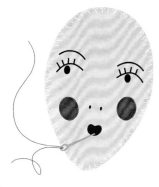

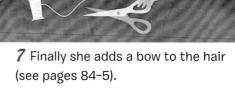

5 Then Doris cuts two small circles from pink felt for the cheeks and a mouth shape from red felt, and stitches them onto the face with tiny running stitches in matching sewing thread. She embroiders the eyebrows and eyelashes in black backstitch, the blue eyes in a circle of chain stitches, and the nostrils with three or four straight stitches worked close together.

6 Next, she slips the face under the V-shaped slit in the hair piece, lightly glues it in place and leaves it to dry. She pins the second hair shape to the back of the face and blanket stitches around the edge using matching thread, being sure to leave a big enough gap at the bottom for her eggs to fit through.

7 Finally she adds a bow to the hair (see pages 84–5).

Doris makes a whole collection of egg-faced friends and is filled with glee. "Don't they look tickety-boo?" she says happily.

Twiggy makes her bed...
and then she lies in it

Materials you will need

- Sewing box or stool
- Tack lifter (forked)
- Long-nose pliers
- Magnetic tack hammer or regular small hammer
- Staple remover
- Screwdriver
- Fabric in five different designs, for interior, exterior, lid, panels, and pillow
- Staple gun with staples no longer than the depth of your panels
- Beading trim/ribbon (optional)
- Foam (if original is worn)
- Felt (if working around hinges)
- Thick card (if your sewing stool has no panels)
- Batting (wadding)
- Glue gun
- Pillow
- Self-cover buttons

Twiggy pads into the studio one sunny morning and discovers Chloe's much-loved sewing stool sitting on the floor. She pussyfoots around it, gives it a curious sniff, and peers inside. She sees sewing needles, cotton reels, buttons, bobbins, a pin cushion... "What's all this stuff doing in this cozy-looking bed?" she thinks.

She throws it all out onto the floor and clambers inside. It's very comfy, which gives Twiggy "paws" for thought. "Perfect...", she purrs. "Well... almost!" It's far too shabby-looking for a classy cat like Twiggy, so she grabs some of the fabric from the shelves and collects some tools. Time for a spot of renovation!

1 She begins by removing all the original fabric, taking care to keep it in one piece so that she can use it as a template for her new fabric. She uses a tack lifter and long-nose pliers to lift up the old fabric, and carefully removes all the upholstery pins and gimp pins with a hammer and a staple remover. If you are able to un-screw the hinges and remove the lid, do so. Twiggy finds that the screws in the hinges of this stool are so old that she doesn't have the right tool to remove them, so she works around them instead.

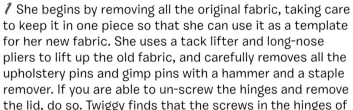

2 She unscrews the legs from underneath and puts the rubber washers to one side. She unscrews the chains at both ends of the hinged lid and sets them aside for later, along with the washers. (She puts pins in the holes where the chain was attached, to remind her where they need to go.) She removes any panels from the inside and outside of the stool, and removes the fabric from these too, until she is left with the plain wooden panels. This all takes a while and requires elbow grease, something Twiggy has never encountered. She takes a cat nap on the sofa before she goes any further.

3 After her nap she feels far more frolicsome and keen to continue with her home improvements. She picks a nice vintage floral fabric for the interior and cuts a piece to size, adding 2 in. (5 cm) extra all around to fold over the edges. She places the fabric inside the stool, making sure she has an even amount of fabric to stretch over the front and back exterior, and staples the front. She removes the pins marking the chain positions when covering, but puts them straight back so she knows where the holes are.

4 She tucks the fabric into the corners. As the stool is curved she has excess fabric, so she folds over the fabric at the edges of the stool to form a pleat and staples it, pushing the staple gun right in to the edges so that it's nice and neat. (If your stool is not curved this won't apply to you.) If you like, you can glue a beading trim or ribbon over the staples to hide them, but they will be hidden once a pillow is put on top.

5 When the fabric meets a hinge, Twiggy tucks it under the groove and pulls it taut to the back. She makes a small diagonal nick away from the hinge at the back, folds a hem to align with it, and secures with a staple. All raw edges will be covered later.

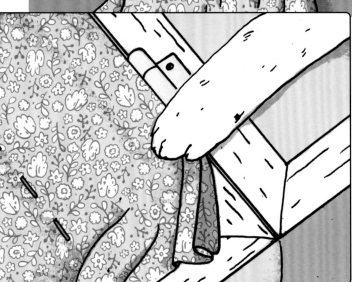

6 Twiggy covers the interior side panels in the same fabric, folding the fabric over neatly at the corners as if she is wrapping a present and securing it with staples at the back; she'll slot these panels back into the stool after she's added the exterior fabric.

7 Next Twiggy uses the main exterior fabric she removed earlier as a template to cut her new fabric, allowing an extra 2 in. (5 cm) of fabric all around. She has chosen a solid turquoise color for this part. She staples from the front along the bottom edge, pulling taut and fold-pleating around the curves. She stretches the fabric over to the back and to the insides of the stool. On the interior corners she folds under the fabric neatly, following the straight edges of the stool.

8 Then she cuts the lid fabric to size, making sure she has enough to cover the foam as well as the lid (at least an extra 3 in./7.5 cm all around). She uses a glue gun to stick the foam on top of the lid, so that it doesn't slip. Next she covers the lid with the fabric as before, folding over the raw edges to the interior of the lid. Again, she marks where the hole goes through the fabric with a pin.

9 As Twiggy works around the hinges, she cuts rectangles of felt to fit around the tops of the hinges, and glues them in place with a glue gun. Then she slots the interior side panels that she covered earlier back into the stool.

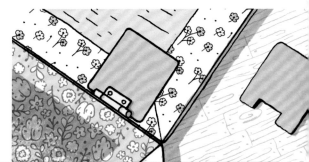

10 Now she is going to cover all her panel pieces. She has three in total—front and back exterior and lid interior. If you don't have any, cut some from thick card. Twiggy cuts batting (wadding) to fit each panel, lays it on top of the relevant panel, then folds over the fabric and staples it at the back, folding and pleating at the curves as neatly and symmetrically as possible.

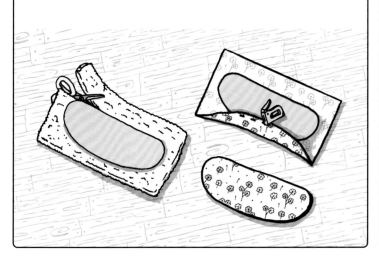

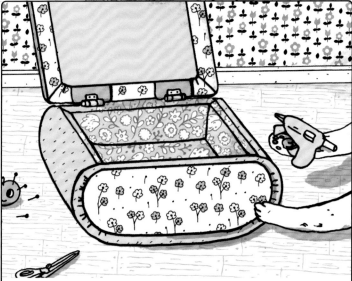

11 When they're all covered, she glues them securely in place with a glue gun, removing the pins in the lid first and making sure that they are properly centered and cover the raw edges of the fabric already stuck down.

12 Next Twiggy re-attaches the chains that hold the lid open. She pierces holes through the interior lid panel using a strong embroidery needle (you could also use a thin screwdriver) and screws one end of each chain into the lid panel. She screws the other ends of the chains into the holes marked with a pin.

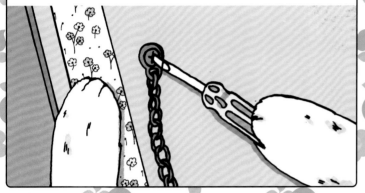

13 Twiggy is getting very excited now because she can see her comfy bed is almost finished. She turns the bed upside down, re-aligns the rubber washers she removed earlier, and staples them in place. She pierces through the fabric under each washer with a strong embroidery needle and screws the legs back on. Then she turns the bed right side up again.

14 Twiggy thinks her new bed is the cat's whiskers, but it's missing something... a pillow! She measures her pillow and cuts fabric ⅜ in. (1 cm) bigger all around for the front. For the back she cuts two pieces measuring two-thirds the length of the front. She folds over a double ⅜-in. (1-cm hem) on one side of each back piece, pins, and sews into place. Then she lays the front pillow piece right side up in front of her with two back pieces right side down on top. She pins them together and sews all the way around, taking a ⅜-in. (1-cm) seam. Then she turns the pillow case right side out.

15 Finally, she covers two self-cover shank buttons in the same fabric as the interior of her bed. To do this she cuts out circles twice the size of the buttons, sews a running stitch around the outside leaving loose thread tails, places a button on the wrong side of the fabric, pulls the thread tails so the fabric gathers around the button, and ties the threads in a double knot. Then she presses the back of the shank button in place and sews one button on at each end of the pillow case. She stuffs her pillow in the case, places it in her bed, gets in, and... Zzzzzzzzzzz!

Shortly after, Chloe walks in ready to start another busy crafting day–and what does she find? A huge mess, with all her sewing materials all over the floor! Threads unraveled, buttons scattered far and wide, a crumpled heap of fabric scraps... who could be responsible?

Gobsmacked, Chloe peers into the depths of what used to be her sewing basket... and sees that someone has moved in! Twiggy snoozes on peacefully, her work complete.

Jammie Dodger Biscuits

Good enough to eat... Jammie Dodgers and other delights!

Materials you will need

- Templates on page 116
- Felt

1 Using the templates on page 116, cut out all the shapes from biscuit-colored felt and red felt (for the raspberry-flavored filling). Cut a heart shape out of one of the biscuit-colored circles and the big splodgy shape.

2 Hand sew the small red felt circle underneath the cut-out heart on the biscuit-colored circle, using four small stitches. Then, using small straight stitches and making sure the hearts are aligned, sew the big splodge with the cut-out heart shape on top. Sew the rest of the splodge shapes around it.

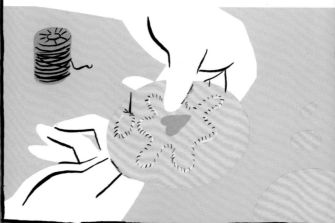

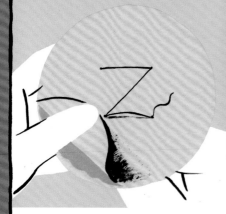

3 Take two more biscuit-colored circles, sandwich the red felt "raspberry filling" in between, and secure with stitches worked in a "Z" shape.

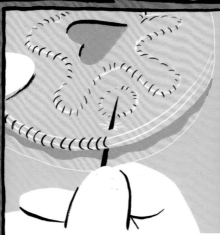

4 Place the layer with the splodges on top and sew it in place with straight stitches all the way around. Then sew the last biscuit-colored circle to the bottom in the same way.

Try making a whole selection of other tasty-looking cakes and biscuits, too. Offer your guests a plate of delicious-looking delights and laugh raucously when they realize they're biting into fakes!

Lotto

A game for 1 or 2 players

Within the boards there are 12 individual designs: apple, buttons, cherries, cotton reel, cup, cupcake, onion, pear, pincushion, scissors, sewing machine, and thimble. Photocopy the 12 pictures twice each onto paper or card and cut out each picture. You can play directly from the book.

Instructions for 1 player: Match up the picture cards with the pictures on the boards.

Instructions for 2 players: Each person plays from one of the boards in the book. The small cards you cut out are then mixed up thoroughly and placed face down in the middle of the table. The person who didn't mix the cards is the first to go and picks any card in the pile. If the card matches a section of his/her board, he/she places it over the matching illustration and has the privilege of picking the next card. This player continues to pick cards until he/she reaches one that does not match his/her board. If the other player needs this card, he/she calls for it and continues to pick and match, as did the previous player. If no one needs the card picked, it is turned face down again and the other player is the next to go.

The play continues until one person has all the sections of his/her board covered with the matching cards and is declared the winner.

Chloë
TELLS YOU HOW...
... to make a feather headdress

Materials you will need

- LOTS OF RIBBONS TO DECORATE THE HEADDRESS AND A LONG PIECE FOR TYING
- TEMPLATE ON PAGE 138
- FELT
- A VARIETY OF FEATHERS
- GLUE GUN AND GLUE STICKS
- TWO BIG BEADS
- CLEAR ADHESIVE TAPE (OPTIONAL)
- TWO SETS OF FEATHER EARRINGS
- EMBELLISHMENTS FOR THE SIDES (BUTTONS OR SHISHA MIRRORS)

1 BEGIN BY MEASURING A PIECE OF RIBBON AROUND YOUR HEAD AND THEN ADD 6 IN. (15 CM) TO EACH SIDE FOR TYING.

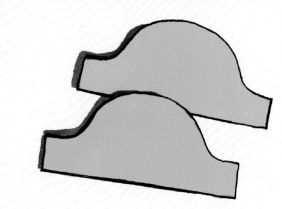

2 USING THE TEMPLATE ON PAGE 138, CUT TWO PIECES OF FELT; ADJUST TO FIT IF NECESSARY. PUT ONE PIECE ASIDE AND LAY THE OTHER ONE IN FRONT OF YOU.

3 GATHER A COLLECTION OF RIBBONS AND LAY THEM OUT FROM BOTTOM TO TOP ACROSS THE FELT IN AN ORDER THAT YOU LIKE. CUT TO SIZE AND STICK THEM IN PLACE WITH FABRIC GLUE.

4 TAKE THE FELT TO YOUR SEWING MACHINE. USING A STRAIGHT STITCH, SEW ALONG THE TOP AND BOTTOM OF EACH RIBBON. THEN ZIG-ZAG STITCH AROUND THE HEADDRESS FROM BOTTOM LEFT TO BOTTOM RIGHT, CLOSE TO THE EDGE.

THIS WILL STOP THE RIBBONS FROM FRAYING AND HELP KEEP YOUR HEADDRESS IN TIP-TOP CONDITION.

5 NOW TAKE YOUR SECOND PIECE OF FELT AND ARRANGE THE FEATHERS ON IT IN YOUR CHOSEN ORDER; TRY TO KEEP MOST OF THE FEATHER STEM WITHIN THE FELT HEADPIECE. USING A GLUE GUN, STICK THE FEATHERS FIRMLY IN PLACE.

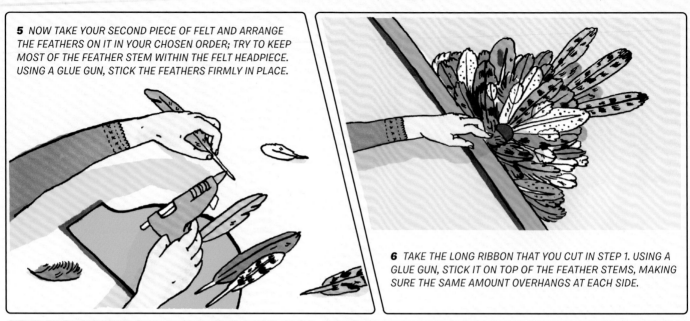

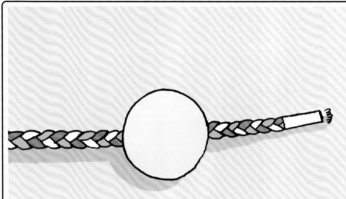

6 TAKE THE LONG RIBBON THAT YOU CUT IN STEP 1. USING A GLUE GUN, STICK IT ON TOP OF THE FEATHER STEMS, MAKING SURE THE SAME AMOUNT OVERHANGS AT EACH SIDE.

7 CHOOSE THREE COLORS OF RIBBON AND CUT TWO 12-IN. (30-CM) STRIPS OF EACH ONE. DIVIDE THEM INTO TWO GROUPS, KNOT THE TOP, AND BRAID (PLAIT) THEM.

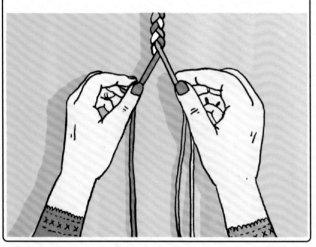

8 THREAD THE UNKNOTTED END THROUGH YOUR BEAD; IF YOU STRUGGLE WITH THIS, IT HELPS TO WRAP ADHESIVE TAPE AROUND THE END BEFORE THREADING IT THROUGH. THEN KNOT THE END OF THE RIBBON.

9 SEW A BRAID TO EACH SIDE OF THE FRONT OF THE HEADDRESS. ADD ANOTHER RIBBON TO EACH SIDE, THEN SEW TWO FEATHER EARRINGS TO EACH RIBBON.

10 USING A GLUE GUN, GLUE THE FRONT PIECE TO THE BACK PIECE.

11 THEN CHOOSE A LONG RIBBON TO WRAP AROUND THE EDGE OF THE HEADDRESS AND HANG DOWN ON EACH SIDE; A FRINGED RIBBON WOULD WORK WELL.

GLUE IN PLACE WITH FABRIC GLUE AND THEN SEW ALL THE WAY AROUND THE PERIMETER OF THE HEADDRESS.

12 ADD EMBELLISHMENTS TO EACH SIDE OF THE HEADDRESS–AND TA-DA!

PUZZLES

Can you find the five hidden thimbles?

Color in the dancers' clothes

Dot to dot

Sewing

Sewing card

Can you spot five differences between the two pictures?

HOOPLA!

Thrifty Thelma and Woolly the Lamb decorate a wall with fabric hoops.

Materials you will need

- Fabric at least 2 in. (5 cm) wider all around than your hoops
- Embroidery hoops of various sizes
- Nails and a hammer

1 Thelma and Woolly are tired of the drab and drearily dull wall in their living room. They've decided to perk it up a bit. They gather lots of different fabrics together and find some embroidery hoops.

2 They position the fabric in the hoop, pull it taut, and screw the hoop tightly closed.

3 They flip the hoop over so that they can see the wrong side of the fabric and dab glue all the way around the rim of the inner ring.

4 They fold the fabric over the inner ring, press it into the glue, and leave to dry. Then they trim off the excess fabric so that it's in line with the hoop.

5 Thelma and Woolly hammer nails into the wall and hang the fabric hoops on them. "How hunky-dory," they say! "Now the wall looks far from boring!"

A MUST HAVE FOR THE MODERN MAN

THE DELUXE FELT BEARD, NOW WITH OPTIONAL MOUSTACHE

CHILLY CHIN? Tired of getting turned away from folk-music clubs? Want that "fully bearded" look, but only have an hour?

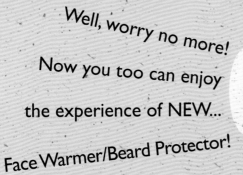

Well, worry no more! Now you too can enjoy the experience of NEW...

Face Warmer/Beard Protector!

This stylish garment exhilarates the skin and safeguards against the cold— there's nothing like it for style and comfort. This man wears his beard with confidence. He feels the benefits. She won't be able to resist!

DESIGNED WITH **YOU** IN MIND ...

Face Warmer / Beard Protector
The finest facial fuzz—with half the fuss!

1 Cut out two beard and two moustache shapes from felt in the color of your choice.

2 Using a freehand machine embroidery foot and a contrasting thread, stitch swirling lines on top of one beard shape. Then stitch lines onto one of the moustaches from one end to the other, following its shape.

3 Lay the moustache shapes wrong sides together and sew around the edge, taking a ⅛-in. (3-mm) seam and leaving a 1½-in. (4-cm) opening for the stuffing. Stuff the moustache, then sew the opening closed.

4 Measure the elastic around your head from ear to ear, pull it slightly taut, and cut to length.

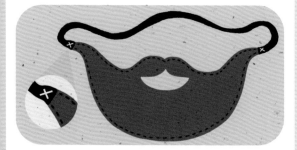

5 Lay the back of the beard on a table in front of you and position one end of the elastic at each top corner. Pin in place and stitch with a criss-cross.

6 Lay the front of the beard right side up on top of the back, and sew the two beard shapes together as you did with the moustache, using a zig-zag stitch for the outside and a straight stitch for the mouth opening.

7 Hand sew the moustache to the beard, above the mouth opening. Place on your face for manly charm and sophistication.

Now nobody will ever suspect you have no chin!

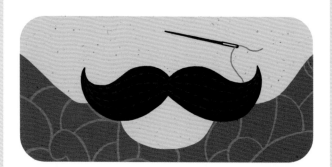

Yours!
Because *you* made it!

She ain't no drag... Chloë's got a

Materials you will need

- Templates on pages 138-39
- Wooden bag handles
- Fusible fleece interfacing
- Outer fabric, lining fabric, and fabric for pocket
- A pile of fabric to cut segments and shapes from

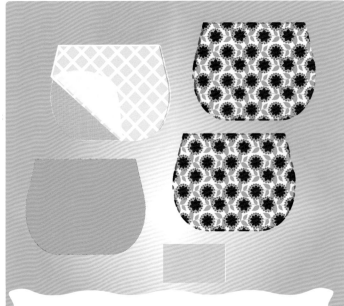

1 Measure the opening in your bag handles and adjust the bag main piece template on page 138 to fit if necessary.

2 Iron the fleece interfacing onto the wrong side of your chosen outer fabric and cut the front and back pieces using your template. Cut two lining pieces and the fabric for the pocket.

3 Next, carefully cut out lots of different shapes from your bundle of fabric—flowers, swirls, paisley patterns and butterflies, or anything that catches your eye. When you have a nice collection, position them on the front of the bag, glue them in place, and leave to dry.

4 Sew around your shapes in threads of your choice, using a freehand machine embroidery foot. You can use a straight stitch, zig-zag stitch, or any sort of stitch you like the look of!

brand new bag

5 Next, fold the pocket fabric in half lengthwise, right sides together, and press. Put the standard presser foot back on your sewing machine and sew a straight stitch all the way around, using a ¼-in. (5-mm) seam allowance and leaving a 1½-in. (4-cm) gap for turning.

6 Clip the corners, then turn the pocket right side out. Fold the unstitched section of seam in on itself and press. Then topstitch along the top of the pocket, starting and finishing ⅜ in. (1 cm) in from each side edge.

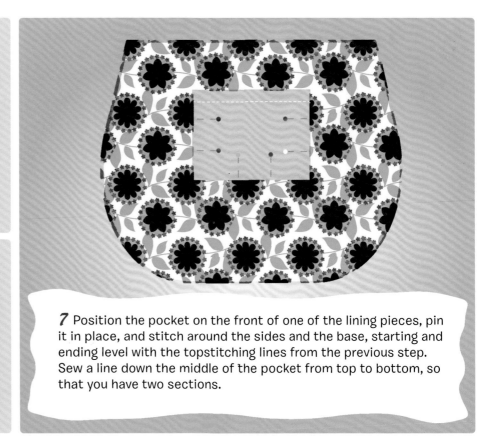

7 Position the pocket on the front of one of the lining pieces, pin it in place, and stitch around the sides and the base, starting and ending level with the topstitching lines from the previous step. Sew a line down the middle of the pocket from top to bottom, so that you have two sections.

8 Place the lining with the pocket and the back of the bag right sides together. Pin along the top straight edge and pin down each side for about 4¾ in. (12 cm) from the top, then sew the pinned sections, taking a ⅜-in. (1-cm) seam. Repeat with the other two pieces. You now have the front and back of your bag: on each one, the top and half the sides are sewn while the bottom is unstitched.

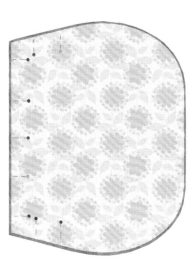

9 Next, open up the un-sewn bottom sections. Lay the front and back linings right sides together and pin together around the unstitched section. Then lay the front and back outer fabrics right sides together and pin.

10 Sew around the pinned sections of the outer fabrics, taking a ⅜-in. (1-cm) seam. Repeat with the pinned sections of the lining fabrics, leaving an opening in the bottom edge big enough for turning. Trim the seam allowances and notch the curves. Turn the bag right side out through the gap in the lining, then slipstitch the opening closed.

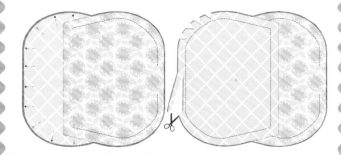

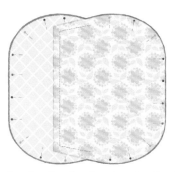

11 Stuff the lining into the bag and press. Then sew a short horizontal reinforcement stitch under the bag opening on each side, ⅜ in. (1 cm) in length.

12 Slot the top of one side of the bag through one of your handles and fold it over to the lining side.

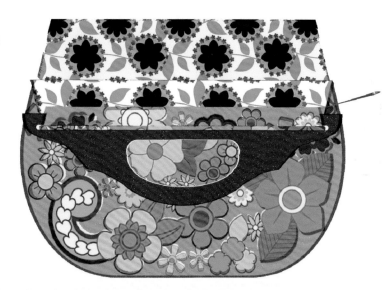

Using a strong thread or doubling over your standard thread, slipstitch the folded edge to the lining. Repeat to attach the other handle.

Fred Bear

Bernadette the lonely bear makes herself a date

Materials you will need

- Templates on pages 129-31
- Fabric for bear's top, ears, and pants
- Felt-red, light brown, black, white, dark brown-for bear's head and facial features
- Ribbon
- Toy stuffing or fabric scraps

Bernadette, or Bernie as she's known to her friends, is lonely. In fact, she *has* no friends these days. Her owner Peggy has grown up and forgotten all about her, so Bernie just sits on a shelf all day, bored out of her stuffing-filled mind.

One afternoon Bernie thinks to herself, "I won't sit here all alone a day longer," and she jumps down onto the bedroom floor.

Like a bear on a mission she searches high and low, in drawers and trinket boxes, at the back of the wardrobe and under the bed, until she's found enough materials. "I'm going to make myself a date," she says aloud. (Not that anyone would hear her-she was the only toy in the room aside from an old Speak 'n' Spell with dying batteries, but Bernie didn't count on that for decent conversation these days!)

1 She finds some scissors, cuts out all her fabric pieces, and then irons them so they're nice and crisp. Then she cuts the head and facial features from felt. She includes a snout with a mouth shape cut out of it and teeth, so her new friend will have a nice smile-a good sense of humor is very important to Bernie.

2 She glues the teeth to the back of the mouth opening in the snout, and then glues the red piece of felt on top. She turns it over and there is a handsome bear mouth smiling back at her.

3 Bernie sticks the nose to the top of the snout and the snout to the front head piece, and draws a line from the nose to the mouth, and whisker marks on either side of the nose. Then she glues on the white felt outer eyes and the pink cheeks.

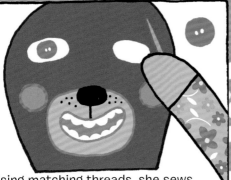

4 Using matching threads, she sews around the snout, nose, outer eyes, and cheeks, then over the drawn lines and whisker marks in black. She leaves the teeth un-stitched, but sews on two bright blue buttons for eyes.

5 She pins the ear pieces right sides together (the fronts of the ears are cut from one of Peggy's old flowery dresses and the backs from brown felt). She sews around the curved edges, leaving the bottom straight edges open; then she notches the curves, turns the ears right side out, and folds each one in half, patterned sides together. Starting from the folded edge, she sews a short line of stitches ⅜ in. (1 cm) from the bottom, then opens out the ears.

6 Next Bernie cuts four pieces of ribbon about 9 in. (22 cm) long. She glues two pieces to the front body and two to the back for the bear's braces, and stitches them in place with matching thread. She likes a man who knows how to dress.

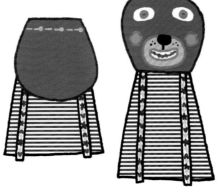

7 Bernie pins the front head and front body pieces right sides together and sews a straight stitch with a ⅜-in. (1-cm) seam allowance, then she presses the seam open.

8 She repeats with the pants and feet, then does the same with all the back pieces.

9 She pins and sews each hand to its accompanying arm, then pins and sews each arm right sides together, with a ⅜-in. (1-cm) seam allowance every time. She turns the arms right side out and stuffs them.

10 Bernie sews the top to the pants, right sides together (see step 7, page 22); then she sews a button to the top of the pants, under each ribbon. She sandwiches the ears and arms in place and pins the back of the bear to the front, right sides together (see steps 9 and 10, page 23). Taking a ⅜-in. (1-cm) seam, she stitches all the way around, leaving a 4-in. (10-cm) gap in one side.

11 She notches all the curves, turns her beautiful beau right side out, stuffs him, and then slipstitches the opening closed. "Oh, my!" she swoons, "you are handsome!"

Fred looks at her with those big blue eyes and she's already fallen under his spell. He adoringly brushes a piece of thread away from her face and swoops her up in his arms for a romantic smooch worthy of an Oscar.

They live happily ever after.

Bumper fun activity pages!

Name that stitch!

Help Jimmy and Harvey by drawing lines to match up the names of these stitching techniques to the correct pictures.

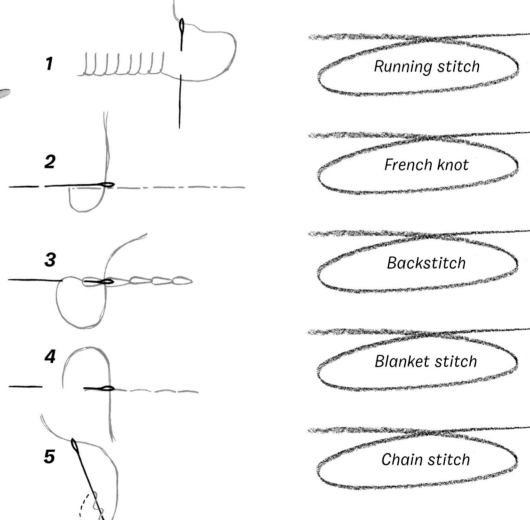

1

2

3

4

5

Running stitch

French knot

Backstitch

Blanket stitch

Chain stitch

Amazing maze!

Cyril the squirrel has lost his collection of nuts! Help him to find them by showing him the way through the maze.

Bertie Badger and the Cockney Sparrow cross-stitch pattern

Cut your aida fabric to the right size and find the center point by folding it lightly into four. Starting in the center, cross-stitch using the color key as your guide. Add detail with straight stitches.

You will need

Aida fabric, needle, scissors, and embroidery floss (thread) in the colors listed below

Color key
- Sky blue
- Brown
- Orange
- Dark brown
- White

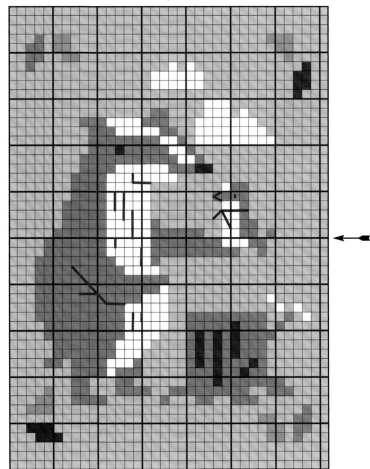

The answers to Name that Stitch are here!

The stitches are: (1) blanket stitch, (2) running stitch, (3) chain stitch, (4) backstitch, and (5) French knot

Chloë

TELLS YOU HOW...

... to make a camera case

Materials you will need

- CAMERA
- FELT IN DARK BROWN, BEIGE, AND BLACK
- BROWN EMBROIDERY FLOSS (THREAD)
- ⅛-IN. (3-MM) RIBBON IN RED, YELLOW, GREEN, AND BLUE
- EXTRA RIBBON FOR FASTENING IN ANY COLOR
- STUFFING OR FABRIC SCRAPS
- A BUTTON IN ANY COLOR

1 FIRST, MEASURE YOUR CAMERA: MEASURE 1¼ TIMES AROUND THE CAMERA, THEN MEASURE THE WIDTH AND LENGTH OF THE TOP AND BASE, AND THE HEIGHT.

2 CUT TWO PIECES OF DARK BROWN FELT MEASURING THE HEIGHT AND 1¼ TIMES THE PERIMETER OF YOUR CAMERA. THEN CUT A STRIP OF BEIGE FELT THE SAME LENGTH BUT TWO-THIRDS THE HEIGHT. ALL PIECES SHOULD HAVE CURVED CORNERS AT ONE END.

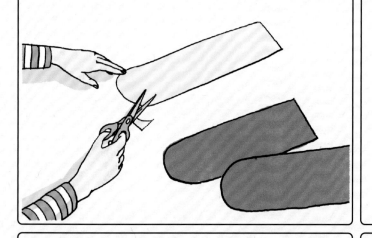

3 CUT A CIRCLE OF BROWN AND A CIRCLE OF BEIGE FELT, WITH A DIAMETER ⅜ IN. (1 CM) LESS THAN THE HEIGHT OF YOUR CAMERA. THEN CUT A HOLE IN THE BEIGE CIRCLE ⅜ IN. (1 CM) SMALLER, SO YOU'RE LEFT WITH A BEIGE RING. PLACE THE BEIGE RING ON TOP OF THE BROWN CIRCLE AND STRAIGHT STITCH ALL THE WAY AROUND.

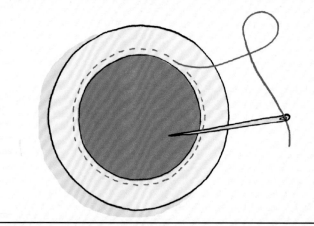

4 MEASURE THE CIRCUMFERENCE OF THE CIRCLE AND CUT ANOTHER STRIP OF BEIGE FELT TO THIS LENGTH AND ⅝ IN. (1.5 CM) HIGH. SEW ONE LONG EDGE OF THE STRIP AROUND THE CIRCLE WITH STRAIGHT STITCHES, THEN SEW THE STRAIGHT ENDS TOGETHER WITH THE SAME STITCH. NOW YOU HAVE A LENS.

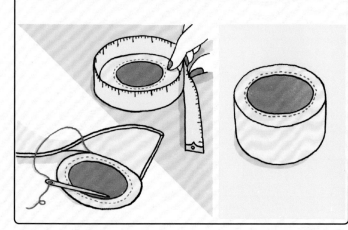

5 WRAP ONE OF THE DARK BROWN FELT STRIPS AROUND YOUR CAMERA 1¼ TIMES, TO WORK OUT THE CENTER OF THE FRONT, WHERE YOUR LENS WILL GO.

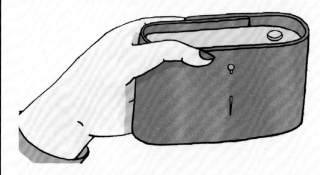

THE STRAIGHT EDGE SHOULD START AT THE BACK ON THE RIGHT-HAND SIDE AND THE CURVED EDGE SHOULD END AT THE CENTER OF THE BACK. MARK THE LENS POSITION WITH A PIN.

6 CUT THE RIBBONS TO HALF THE HEIGHT OF YOUR CAMERA AND POSITION THEM TO THE LEFT OF WHERE THE LENS WILL BE. THE RIBBONS SHOULD OVERLAP AT THE TOP; WHEN THE BEIGE STRIP IS ADDED, THE BOTTOMS WILL BE TUCKED UNDERNEATH.

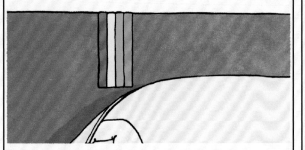

LIGHTLY GLUE THE RIBBONS IN PLACE, FOLDING THE TOPS OVER TO THE BACK, AND STITCH IN PLACE WITH MATCHING THREADS.

7 NOW GLUE THE BEIGE STRIP ON TOP, ALIGNING THE BOTTOM EDGE WITH THE BOTTOM OF THE BROWN STRIP AND COVERING THE BOTTOM EDGES OF THE RIBBONS. STRAIGHT STITCH ALONG THE TOP EDGE OF THE BEIGE STRIP IN BROWN THREAD.

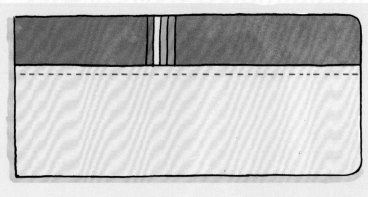
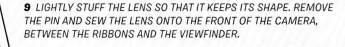

8 CUT A SMALL RECTANGLE FROM BLACK FELT, ⅜ IN. (1 CM) SHORTER THAN THE VISIBLE STRIP OF BROWN AND 1½ TIMES LONGER THAN ITS OWN HEIGHT. POSITION IT TO THE RIGHT OF WHERE THE LENS WILL BE AND STRAIGHT STITCH IN WHITE THREAD. NOW YOU HAVE A VIEWFINDER.

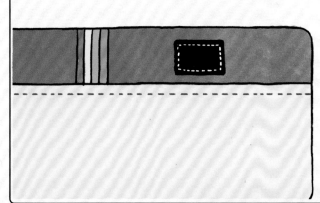

9 LIGHTLY STUFF THE LENS SO THAT IT KEEPS ITS SHAPE. REMOVE THE PIN AND SEW THE LENS ONTO THE FRONT OF THE CAMERA, BETWEEN THE RIBBONS AND THE VIEWFINDER.

10 CUT ANOTHER PIECE OF ⅛-IN. (3-MM) RIBBON IN YOUR CHOSEN COLOR ABOUT 2 IN. (5 CM) IN LENGTH, FOLD IT INTO A LOOP, AND POSITION IT TO THE BACK OF THE CAMERA, AT THE CURVED END.

GLUE THE OTHER DARK BROWN FELT STRIP FROM STEP 2 TO THE BACK OF THE FRONT PIECE, MAKING SURE THAT ALL THE EDGES LINE UP AND THE RIBBON ENDS ARE SANDWICHED IN BETWEEN.

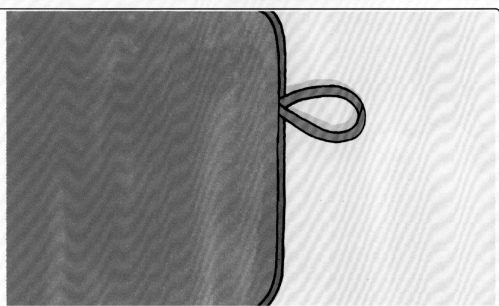

11 CUT ONE PIECE OF BEIGE AND ONE PIECE OF BROWN FELT FOR THE TOP AND BOTTOM OF THE CAMERA CASE, WITH ONE STRAIGHT END AND ONE CURVED END. LAY THEM ON THE BACK OF YOUR CAMERA CASE, SO THAT THE STRAIGHT EDGES LINE UP WITH THE STRAIGHT EDGES OF THE CAMERA CASE, AND BEIGE IS ALIGNED WITH BEIGE AND BROWN WITH BROWN. ATTACH TOGETHER WITH STRAIGHT STITCHES ALONG THE LONG STRAIGHT OUTER EDGES.

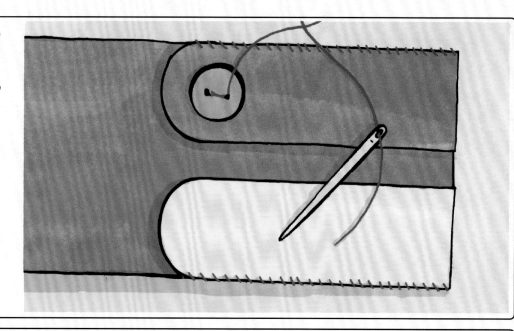

12 THEN LIFT UP THE STRIPS SO THAT THEY ARE AT RIGHT ANGLES TO THE CAMERA CASE FRONT. FOLD THE CURVED END OF THE CAMERA CASE TOWARD THE STRIPS, SO THAT THE CURVED ENDS MEET, AND CONTINUE STITCHING AROUND UNTIL YOU REACH THE STRAIGHT EDGES OF THE TOP AND BASE FELT STRIPS. LEAVE THESE ENDS UN-STITCHED TO SLOT YOUR CAMERA THROUGH.

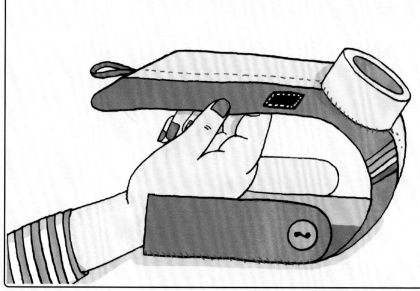

13 SEW UP ALL RAW EDGES WITH A BLANKET STITCH (SEE PAGE 113), MATCHING THE THREAD TO THE FELT. FINALLY, MARK WHERE THE LOOP OF THE RIBBON MEETS THE BACK OF THE CAMERA CASE AND SEW A BUTTON TO THE BACK FOR A FASTENING.

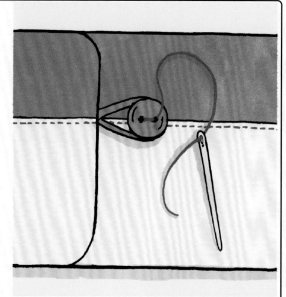

Patchwork QUILT

Miss Wibbles feels chilly, so she makes herself a blanket !

Materials you will need

- Fabric for squares
- Rotary cutter, cutting mat, and quilter's ruler (optional)
- Fabric for backing
- Masking tape
- Quilt batting (wadding)
- Hair clips or quilting clips
- Quilting needle (optional)
- A walking foot (if using a sewing machine)
- Fabric for binding (or bias binding 2¼ in. /6 cm wide)

1 First, Miss Wibbles decides how big her quilt should be. She'd like it big enough to snuggle under and settles on 40 x 20 in. (100 x 150 cm). She wants her squares to be 4 in. (10 cm) when sewn, so to allow for the seams she cuts out 150 squares measuring 5 x 5 in. (12 x 12 cm) from different fabrics.

2 When she's finished cutting out all her squares, she lays them down on the floor in an order she likes, in 15 rows of 10 squares each. Working from top to bottom, she picks up all the squares from each row in turn, puts them in a neat pile ready for sewing, and labels each pile with the row number, so that she can keep them in order.

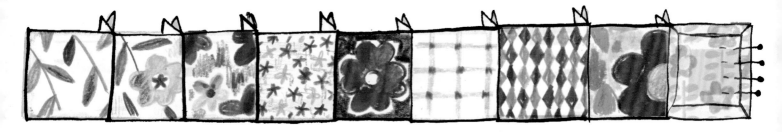

3 She pins the first two squares of Row 1 right sides together, and sews, taking a ½-in. (1-cm) seam allowance. Then she does the same with the next square, and then the next, until her first row of 10 squares is a strip of fabric.

4 She repeats step 3 with the remaining piles of squares until she has 15 strips. She presses all the seams to one side, facing in opposite directions in alternate rows. Then she pins the first two strips right sides together and sews them, taking a ½-in. (1-cm) seam allowance. She does the same with the remaining strips until she has a large piece of fabric 10 squares across and 15 squares down.

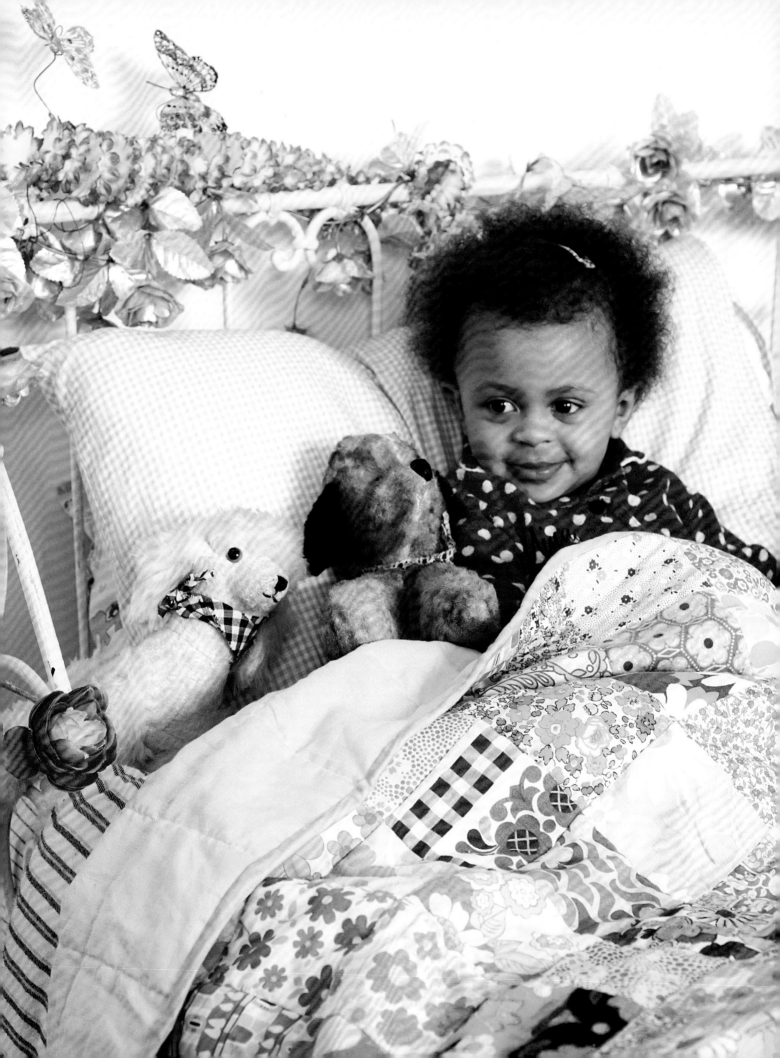

5 She presses all the seams to one side, facing in opposite directions in alternate rows. Then she cuts her backing fabric about 2 in. (5 cm) bigger all around than the quilt top. She presses the backing fabric and lays it right side down on the floor, smoothing the fabric nicely. She sticks each side of the backing fabric to the floor with small strips of masking tape to keep it neatly in place.

6 Next she cuts her batting (wadding) a little smaller than her backing fabric and lays this in the center of the backing. Finally, she places the top of the quilt, right side up, on top of the backing and batting, making sure the backing and batting overhang by the same amount on all four sides.

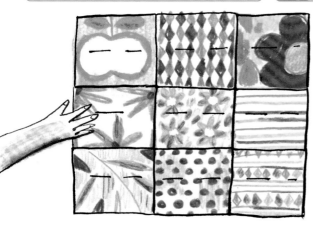

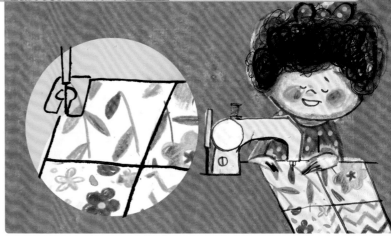

7 Miss Wibbles takes a needle and thread and bastes (tacks) the quilt through all three layers, starting from the center and working outward, smoothing the fabric as she goes. She works by splitting the quilt into quarters, and bastes each quarter at a different angle. The first quarter is basted vertically, the second horizontally, the third vertically, and the fourth horizontally again.

8 Next she takes to her sewing machine and uses her walking foot to "stitch in the ditch" (sew along the seam lines), starting from the top in the center down to the bottom. She then rotates the quilt 90 degrees and does the same again, so that she has a giant cross sewn into the quilt. Then she continues, top to bottom, side to side, until she has sewn the entire quilt. She trims the backing and batting level with the top of the quilt.

9 She then measures around all four sides of the quilt and adds another 16 in. (40 cm). She cuts strips of fabric on the bias 2¼ in. (6 cm) wide, until she has enough.

10 She pins the first two binding strips together at 90° and stitches across diagonally, ¼ in. (6 mm) from the edge. Then she trims the seam allowance and presses the seam open. She repeats this until all the strips have been joined together into one long length.

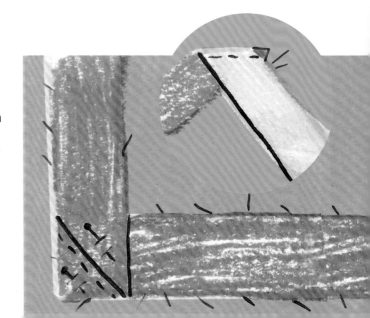

11 With wrong sides together, she presses the entire strip in half along its length. Starting 8 in. (20 cm) in from the end of the strip, aligning the raw edges of the binding and the quilt, she pins the binding to the edges of the top side of the quilt.

12 When she gets to the corner, she folds the binding away from the quilt at an angle of 90°.

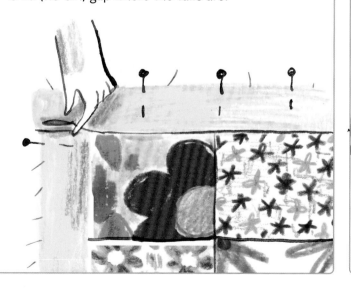

13 She folds the binding back on itself, and pins it to the next side. She continues until she has pinned binding to all four sides of the quilt and has two unpinned tails left. Taking a ¼-in. (6-mm) seam, she sews all the way around, stopping ¼ in. (6 mm) before and after each corner and leaving a 3-in. (7.5-cm) gap where the tails are.

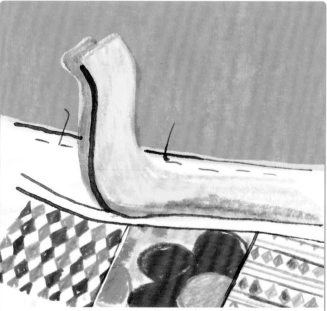

14 Miss Wibbles trims the tails and folds them so that the folded edges meet, and marks the spot with a pencil.

15 She marks where the folded eges meet, then pins the strips together close to the edge and sews along the pin line. Then she trims the seam to ¼ in. (6 mm), presses it open, and then continues her line of stitching across the bias to join them up.

16 Next, she flips the binding over the back of the quilt and keeps it in place with hair clips, making sure it covers the previous binding stitches. At the corners, she folds and tuck the fabric over carefully to get neat mitered corners.

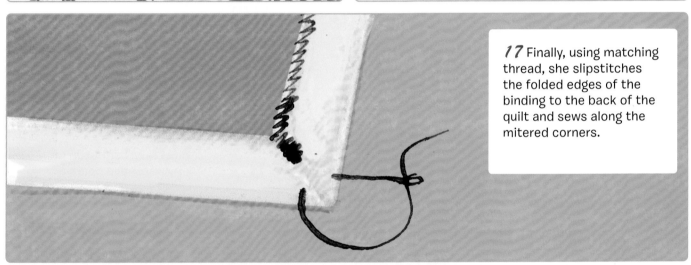

17 Finally, using matching thread, she slipstitches the folded edges of the binding to the back of the quilt and sews along the mitered corners.

Miss Wibbles eagerly throws the finished quilt onto her bed, jumps under it, and falls asleep, feeling as snug as a bug in a rug. Zzzzzzzzz...

FELT BALL GARLAND

Hilda decides to spruce things up a bit

Materials you will need

- A towel
- Wool tops for felting
- A bottle of warm soapy water
- A bowl of clean water
- Embroidery floss (thread)

1 Hilda lays down a towel to soak up any water that might spill and grabs a handful of wool. She separates the fibers out evenly, so that there are no heavy clumps, and lays it over the palm of her paw.

2 She takes her bottle of soapy water and pours a couple of glugs over the wool.

3 Hilda then squishes the soap into the fibers and scrunches the wool from the center until it begins to gather into a ball.

4 Very gently Hilda rolls the wool in the palms of her paws until it starts to take shape. She keeps rolling, round and round...

5 After a few minutes, the felt ball starts to form into a firm shape. Then she dips it into clean water to rinse it, and gently squeezes out the excess water. She carries on rolling and rinsing until the ball feels dense.

If you notice a crack in the wool while you're rolling and rinsing the ball, take another smaller layer of wool and repeat the process again; this smoothes it all out nicely.

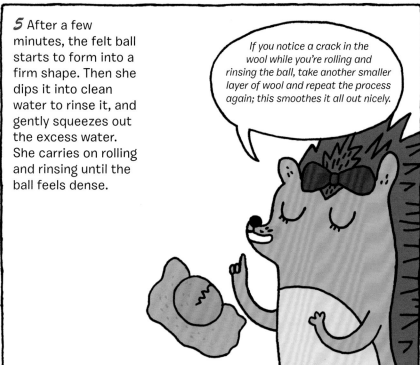

6 Once she has built up a nice stockpile of colorful felt balls, she threads them onto a piece of embroidery floss (thread), ties a loop at each end, and hangs them on the wall.

She discovers something very effective for enhancing her prickles, too...

Raise the curtain

This Scandinavian-inspired project is good for hiding clutter under sinks or as an alternative to boring cupboards.

Materials you will need

- Fabric for the curtain and appliqué pieces
- Two ribbons the width of your curtain
- Templates on pages 123-27
- Fusible bonding web
- Curtain wire with hooks and eyes

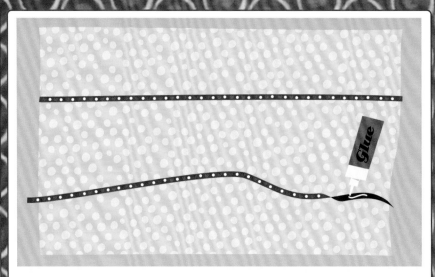

1 Begin by measuring the space under your sink and cut your fabric to size, adding 1 in. (2.5 cm) to the right and left edges, 3 in. (8 cm) to the top edge, and 2 in. (5 cm) to the bottom edge. Press so that the fabric is nice and crisp.

2 Taking the top and bottom hems into account, divide the height of the curtain by three, then pin or glue your ribbons across the width, making sure they are evenly spaced. Sew along each ribbon edge with a straight stitch and matching thread.

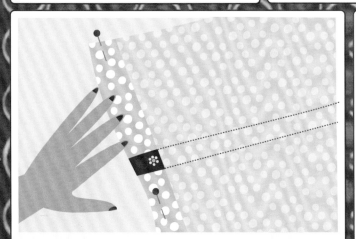

3 Next, fold over the left and right sides of the curtain by ½ in. (12 mm) twice and pin in place. Machine stitch. Repeat at the top and bottom of the curtain, folding the fabric over by 1½ in. (4 cm) and 1 in. (2.5 cm) respectively each time.

4 Iron fusible bonding web onto your chosen appliqué fabrics and cut out the shapes using the templates on pages 123–27. If you can cut out elements such as leaves or flower from your fabrics, do so.

5 Following the manufacturer's instructions, apply the cut-out shapes to the curtain, evenly spaced and slightly floating above the ribbons and the bottom of curtain.

6 Machine stitch around your pieces in threads of your choice. Use decorative stitches for the cherry stalks and the flower stems.

7 Finally, thread a wire cord with metal eyes (loops) attached to the ends through the top casing of the curtain. Screw in the hooks under either side of your sink and hook the curtain on.

Bring the curtain down.

Follow the Thread

Oh, dear!
Wendy has got her cotton reels in an awful tangle!

Can you find which thread is attached to her sewing needle?

The Cockney Sparrow makes a dickory dock*

Materials you will need

- 30-cm (12-in.) embroidery hoop
- Fabric strips
- Glue gun
- Felt
- Small piece of patterned fabric
- Templates on page 122
- Wool tops to make felt balls
- Embroidery needle and floss (thread)
- Ribbon
- Toy filling
- Clock hands and mechanism
- Tracing paper and pencil
- Hammer and nail

'Allo, me old chinas*! I never know what the Harry Lime* is around 'ere, so I'm going to show you how to make a smashin' fabric dickory* using yer own two 'ands and very little bread*. Some folk would have it that you should buy everything new. They're telling porkies*! Cast your minces* over 'ere.

Dickory–"Hickory dickory dock", a line from a child's nursery rhyme = clock
Old china–"china plate" = mate
Harry Lime = time
Bread–"bread and honey" = money
Porkies–"porky pies" = lies
Minces–"mince pies" = eyes

1 Geoff Hurst* take yer embroidery 'oop: it should be in one piece with the screw fastenin' in and a gap big enough to fit a monkey's tail* through. This is where it'll 'ang from.

2 Cut strips of fabric about 2 in. (5 cm) wide. Put a dollop of glue on the top of yer 'oop and stick the end of a strip of fabric to it: mind yer fingers, it don't 'alf get mustard*! Wrap it tightly around until you get to the end of the strip and glue that end to the 'oop, too. Keep doing this until you've covered the whole 'oop two or three times.

Geoff Hurst (British footballer) = first
Monkey–"monkey's tail" = nail

Mustard –"mustard pot" = hot

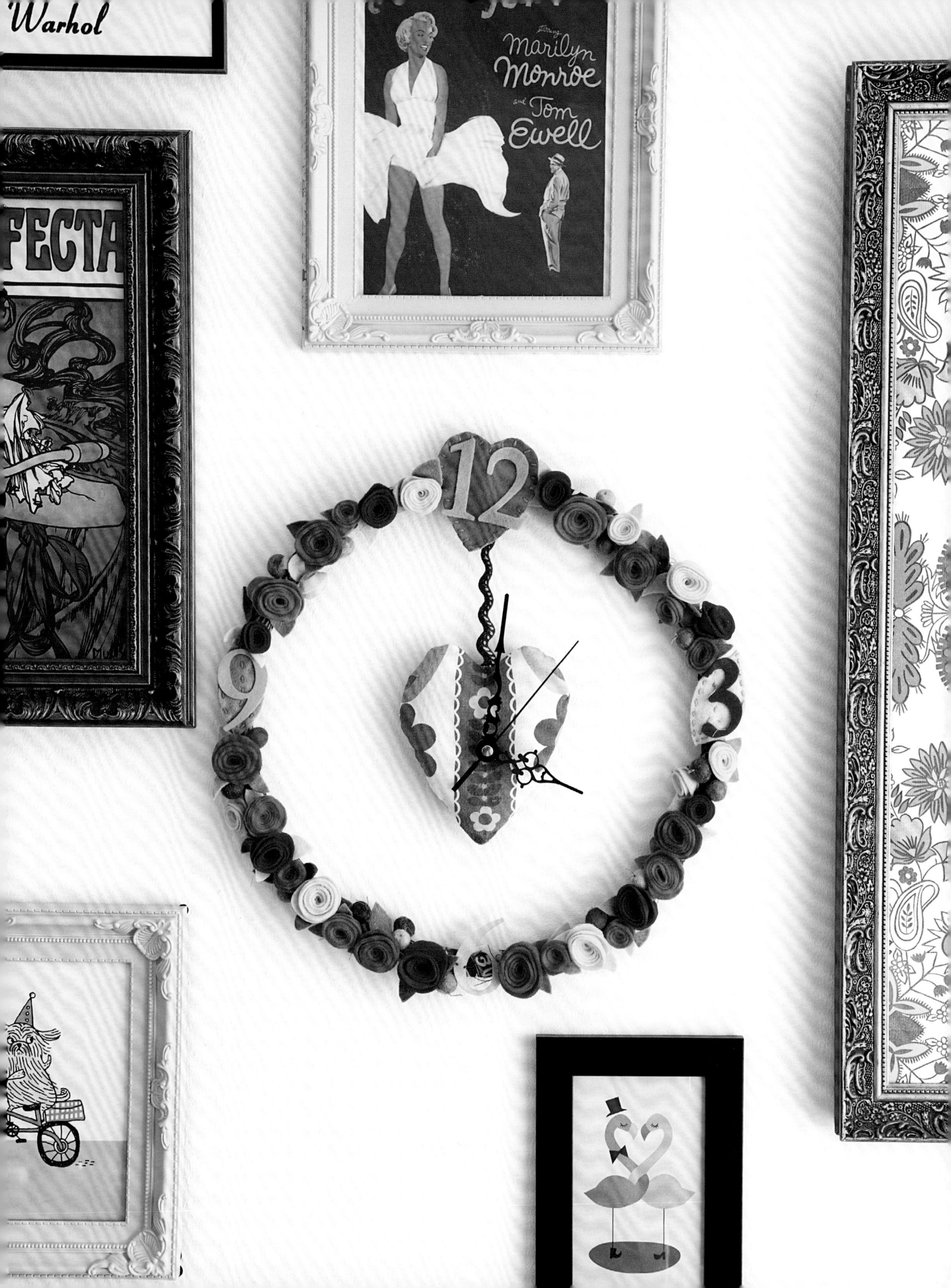
Warhol
Marilyn
Monroe
and Tom
Ewell
FECTA
12
9
3

3 We want to cover our 'oop in lots of charmin' little roses. Choose four colors of felt for the flowers and another four for the leaves. To make a rose, cut out a circle from yer felt, then cut that circle into a spiral. Start gluing from the outside point and curl it up, sticking the last bit to the bottom of the spiral. Then cut two leaf shapes and glue them to the bottom. Make enough in two different sizes to go around the whole 'oop, cut extra leaves to sew around it, and put that little lot to one side.

Bish, bash, bosh*–that's yer roses all done!

Bish, bash, bosh = indicating the completion of a task with efficiency.

4 Then make little felt balls from wool, about ½ in. (1 cm) in diameter (see pages 66–7). You'll need about 10–15 in total. These are yer decorations; you'll be needing these later.

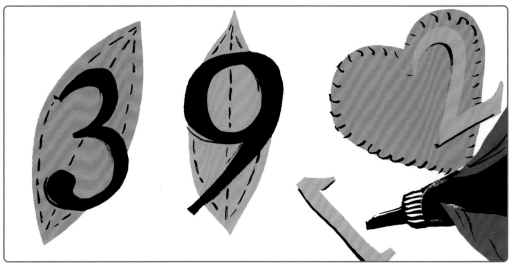

5 Cut out numbers 3, 6, 9, and 12 from yer felt. Then cut out two leaf shapes and sew a running stitch around the edge and down the stem in a contrasting embroidery floss (thread). Glue the number 3 onto one leaf and the number 9 onto another. Then cut out a lovely romantic heart shape, blanket stitch (see page 113) around the outside, and glue the number 12 onto it.

6 Divide yer 'oop into quarters at 45°, 90°, 180°, and 360° and sew on the numbers 3, 6, and 9. We'll save the number 12 until the end. Now sew on yer roses, felt balls, and any extra leaves all the way around, leaving loose ends of thread 'anging 'ere and there to give it a charmin', homespun look.

Cor blimey*, it's starting to look a treat and no mistake!*

Cor blimey = An exclamation of surprise
And no mistake = Added to the end of something you say to emphasize it

7 For the mechanism, cut one large heart from felt and one from another fabric. You might need to adapt the template to fit your mechanism, but it should fit most.

8 Trace around the back of the clock mechanism where the battery and dial are, and cut it out. Position the mechanism and yer template in the center of the felt heart, then draw around the template and cut that shape out of the heart. Don't cut out too much at first: you can always cut more away if you need to.

Ham and cheesy* does it!

....

Ham and cheesy = easy

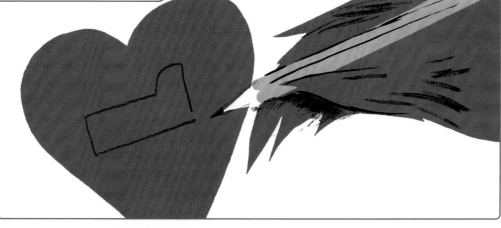

9 Cut a ribbon about 8 in. (20 cm) long and position one end so it pokes over the center of the top of the heart. Pin the hearts right sides together and sew around the edges, leaving a gap big enough to fit the mechanism through. Notch the curves, but don't turn right side out yet.

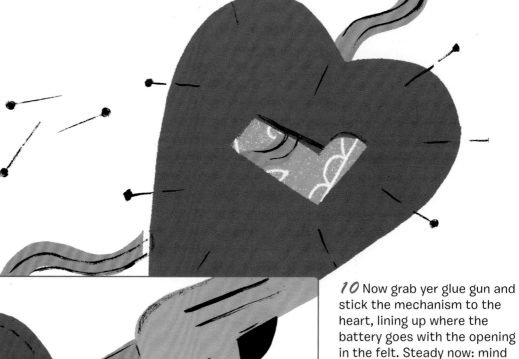

10 Now grab yer glue gun and stick the mechanism to the heart, lining up where the battery goes with the opening in the felt. Steady now: mind you don't get glue on the front of the heart or in the battery compartment. Remove the metal nut and washer, but leave the rubber washer in place.

11 Turn the heart with the mechanism attached right side out, mark where the movement at the front of the mechanism will go, and cut a hole big enough for it to poke through. Lightly stuff the heart and slipstitch it closed. Lovely jubbly!

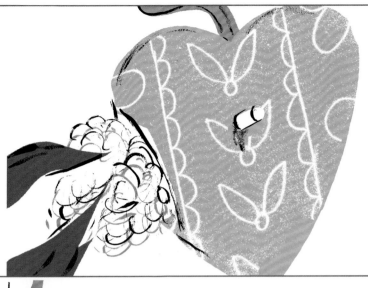

12 Re-attach the metal washer and nut onto the spindle and tighten lightly. Then fit the hour 'and pointing to 12 o'clock, then the minute 'and also pointing to 12 o'clock, and last but not least attach the second 'and to the pin in the center of the movement. Peer at it sideways to make sure the 'ands aren't going to collide.

13 Now attach the heart to the 'oop by looping the ribbon around the 'oop fastenin', making sure the heart will 'ang in the center of the 'oop; trim the ribbon if needs be. Secure the ribbon with a couple of stitches, then sew the heart with the number 12 on top. Job's a good 'un*!

Can you Adam and Eve it? That was a lemon*! You didn't break the iron *, you still 'ave bangers* in yer pocket and you've got a blinding* dickory to boot*.*

14 All that's left to do is 'ang the clock on a monkey through the 'oop fastenin' behind the number 12, insert the battery, and set your new dickory to the right Harry Lime.

Job's a good 'un = an expression of approval; good job, well done

Adam and Eve = believe
Lemon–"lemon squeezy" = easy
Iron–"iron tank" = bank

Bangers–"bangers and mash" (sausage and mashed potato) = cash

Blinding = wonderful/awesome
To boot = in addition

You know you're a cute little toy maker....

FOXY LADY!

Hello, how do you do? I'm going to show you how to make a foxy lady (like me).

Materials you will need

- Templates on pages 116-19
- Fabrics and felts
  - White felt for face and tail ends
  - Orange fabric for face, back of head, back of ears, arms, and tail
  - Fabric for front of ears
  - Brown felt for nose
  - Pink felt for cheeks
  - Blue fabric for eyes
  - Two fabrics for legs and shoes
  - Dress and collar fabric
- Toy filling or fabric scraps
- Embroidery floss (thread) for laces
- Interfacing (optional)

1 Cut out all your fabric pieces and press them. If you're not using felt for the orange part of my face, you will need to cut the bigger size and tuck the extra fabric under to keep it from fraying.

2 Glue or pin the orange part of my face to the white, fold under the fabric from my eyebrow arches to the end of my snout, and press. Using matching thread, sew over the hem, about ¼ in. (6 mm) from the edge.

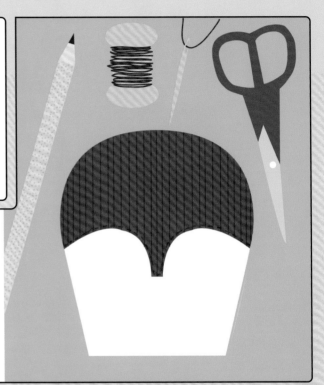

3 Then glue on my felt nose and rosy cheeks. Draw my eyes and lovely lashes, and my mouth and shiny teeth with pencil or a vanishing fabric marker pen, and glue on the blue parts of my eyes.

Take it slow, there's no need to rush!

4 You might choose to iron on a mediumweight interfacing to the back of my face to help with this part. Sew over the eyes and mouth with black thread using a freehand machine embroidery foot, as if you were coloring it in with a pencil. Then sew around the nose and cheeks with matching thread.

5 Pin the two collar pieces right sides together and sew around the curved side with a presser foot. Notch the curves, turn right side out, and press.

6 Lay the front of the dress right side up in front of you with the collar on top, aligning the raw edge of the collar with the top of the dress.

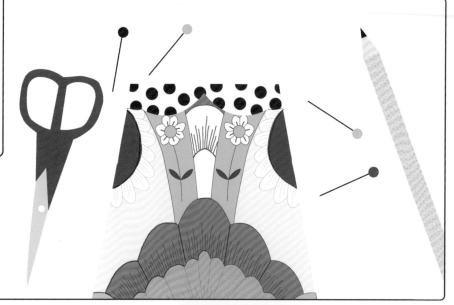

7 Lay my face right side down, aligning the neck with the top of the dress. Pin and sew, taking a ⅜-in. (1-cm) seam, then press the collar down and the seam flat. You might want to work a small stitch by hand at each side of the collar to keep it flat. Then sew the back of my head to the back of the dress.

8 Next, pin my pointy ears right sides together and sew around them, taking a ¼-in. (6-mm) seam and leaving the bottom edge open. Notch the curves, then turn them right side out. Do the same thing with my arms.

9 Then pin or glue my white tail ends to the tops of my orange tails and sew over the jagged ends in white thread. Then pin the tail pieces right sides together and sew around them, taking a ¼-in. (6-mm) seam and leaving the end open. Notch the curves and turn right side out. Stuff my tail.

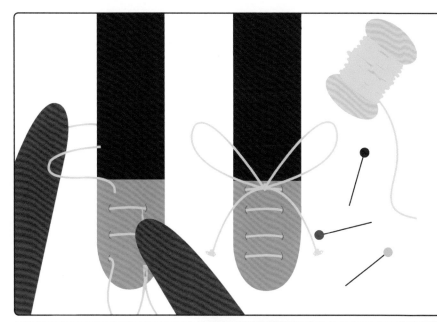

10 Pin and sew my feet to my legs and press the seams flat. Then pin and sew my legs and arms together, right sides facing, and turn right side out. Stuff my arms and legs. For the laces, thread a needle with embroidery floss (thread); starting at the top of the foot, where the laces will be tied and leaving a long tail, sew three straight lines and come back up to the opposite side of where you started. Cut the tail the same length as the first and tie in a bow. Knot the ends so that they don't unravel.

11 Place my ears, arms, and legs on top of the right side of my face and body, and lay the back of me on top, right side down, so that my limbs are sandwiched in the middle. Make sure the ends of all my limbs and ears are poking over the edges slightly, and pin everything in place.

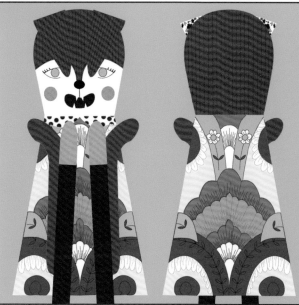

12 Taking a ⅜-in. (1-cm) seam and leaving a 4-in. (10-cm) gap in the side of my dress for turning, sew all the way around. Trim all the seam allowances and notch all the curves, then carefully pull all my limbs through so that I'm right side out.

13 Before you stuff my body, turn to the back of my dress, measure about 1½ in. (4 cm) up from the bottom and mark a line the same height as the open end of my tail. With sharp scissors, carefully cut the line without going through to the front of my dress. Slot the end of my tail through the opening, fold over the open edges of where you cut the dress, and slipstitch it to the tail securely with doubled thread. Fill me with stuffing and slipstitch the opening in my dress closed.

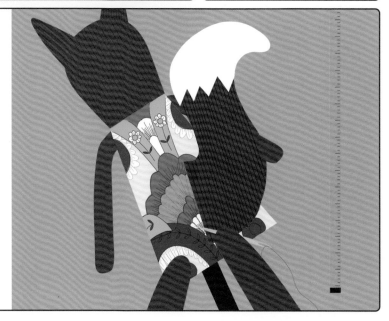

Chloë

TELLS YOU HOW...

... to make multi-purpose bows

Materials you will need

- FABRIC
- CROCODILE CLIPS OR SHOE CLIPS (OPTIONAL)
- HOT GLUE GUN (OPTIONAL)

1 CUT FABRIC TO THE SIZE YOU REQUIRE. (THE HEIGHT WILL BE HALF THE LENGTH OF THE WIDTH.)

FOR A STANDARD-SIZED BOW, CUT A PIECE MEASURING 9 X 4½ IN. (24 X 12 CM). THEN CUT A SMALLER PIECE FOR THE MIDDLE MEASURING 1¼ X 2½ IN. (3 X 6 CM).

2 FOLD THE LONG EDGES OF THE LARGER PIECE IN TO MEET IN THE CENTER AND PRESS. THEN FOLD THE SHORT EDGES IN TO MEET IN THE CENTER AND PRESS.

3 NEXT, PINCH IN THE MIDDLE AS IF YOU ARE BRINGING THE LONG EDGES TOGETHER, SO THAT THE SIDES WITH THE FOLDS ARE FACING INWARD.

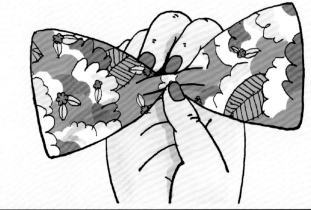

4 THEN FOLD THE LONG EDGES UP TO THE MIDDLE SO THAT YOU CAN SEE THREE FOLDED "LIPS." STITCH IN PLACE, USING MATCHING THREAD.

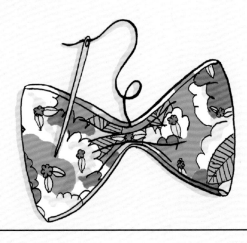

5 FOLD OVER THE LONG EDGES OF THE SMALLER FABRIC PIECE IN THE SAME WAY AS IN STEP 2, THEN FOLD THE SHORT ENDS OVER BY ⅜ IN. (1 CM) AND PRESS.

6 TO ATTACH THE BOW TO A SHOE CLIP, OPEN UP THE CLIP AND STITCH OR GLUE IT TO THE MIDDLE OF THE BOW.

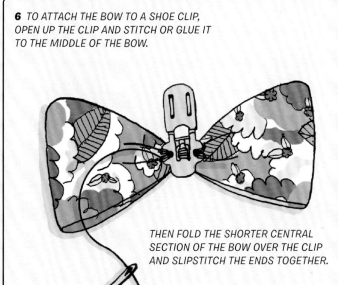

THEN FOLD THE SHORTER CENTRAL SECTION OF THE BOW OVER THE CLIP AND SLIPSTITCH THE ENDS TOGETHER.

7 TO ATTACH THE BOW TO A CROCODILE CLIP, SEW THE SHORTER CENTRAL SECTION OF THE BOW OVER THE MIDDLE OF THE BOW, SLIPSTITCH THE ENDS TOGETHER, AND CLIP THE CROCODILE CLIP THROUGH THE MIDDLE FOLD.

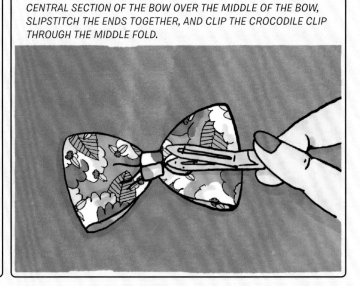

She's a Pinboard Wizard!

For list makers and inspiration takers

Materials you will need

- Frame/vintage picture—preferably with no glass
- Utility or craft knife
- Tack lifter and pliers (optional)
- Cork sheet the same size as your frame
- Batting (wadding)
- Base fabric (this won't be seen)
- Fabrics for appliqué
- Templates on pages 132-33
- Ribbon
- Appliqué foot
- Double-sided tape (optional)
- Staple gun with staples no thicker than the backing board
- Picture framing tape (optional)

1 If you've chosen a vintage picture with no glass, begin by removing the picture and backing board from the frame by cutting the tape at the back with a utility or craft knife. If it has tacks, remove them with a tack lifter and pliers. If you've chosen a standard frame, remove the glass and backing board.

2 Use the backing board as a template to cut the cork sheet to size with sharp scissors. Cut the batting (wadding) the same size. Now cut your base fabric 3 in. (7.5 cm) wider on all sides (you won't see this fabric).

3 Choose fabrics for the background, thought bubble, hair, nails, face and arm, facial features, and sleeve.

4 Adjust the size of the templates on pages 132-33 to fit your chosen frame, and cut out all your separate pieces from the fabrics. Place them on the base fabric, leaving space around the edges of the design so that you can fold the base fabric over the edges of the backing board. Lightly glue everything in place, then draw on the facial features.

5 Pin the batting (wadding) to the back of the fabric, then take to your sewing machine and use a freehand machine embroidery foot to sew over the design in threads of your choice.

6 With the feed dogs up and using an appliqué foot, sew around the thought bubble with a decorative stitch. Add a ribbon to the end of the sleeve for extra detail. Then remove the pins.

7 Next, lay the cork sheet on top of the backing board; you can keep it in place with double-sided tape if that helps. Lay the fabric on top, backing side down. Lay the frame on top to make sure you have it aligned correctly. Trim off any excess batting (wadding) so that it's less bulky for the next step.

8 Stretch the fabric over the backing board and staple it at the back. Fold the corners over neatly as if you're wrapping a present.

9 Push the picture back into the frame securely. Then re-cover the edges with picture framing tape if you removed any at the start.

Hang on a wall and pin up all your "must-do" lists and things that inspire you.

You sure make a mean pinboard!

Continued...

11
Down the street they hopped and jumped,
Laughing as into each other they bumped.
Some got excited and started to hump,
Hidden from view behind a huge tree stump.

12
Three days passed, they multiplied fast.
They lived hidden from humans as bunny outcasts.
But the rabbits thrived as four decades went by.
Their numbers rocketed, their population sky high.

13
In this new era they just didn't belong,
They missed the groovy '60s, its color and song.
This modern way of life felt totally wrong.
They settled on a clever scheme before too long.

14
They arranged to hook up in an old circus tent,
The meeting was loud, it was quite an event.
A way to escape they would have to invent,
For the lives they were living they'd begun to resent.

15
They worked very hard on days one to fifteen,
Serene at the thought of what was foreseen.
At the end of that day in aquamarine,
Sat a splendid and shiny new huge time machine!

16
This was to be a great final frontier,
Into the machine entered the first pioneer.
Whether this was to work was still somewhat unclear,
But they all piled in and put it straight into gear,

Bunnies...

17

Soon they were back in the time of the '60s once more,
With the free love and color they all adored.
No humans noticed, they all walked past blind,
From psychedelic substances they were out of their minds!

18

When they reached the house the bunnies hopped indoors,
Back on that first Sunday in '64.
They all squeezed back into Mildred's bedroom,
The time she'd be back from church did loom.

19

She walked back in her house feeling worry and fright,
She stood awestruck at this mind-boggling sight.
From floor to ceiling, from window to door,
There were more bunnies than ever before.

20

Though Mildred was shocked, she softened her heart.
The rabbits rejoiced, they'd loathed being apart.
She had to learn to accept these friends,
And they all lived happily (though squashed) in the end.

Make a band on your hand!

Introducing the portable popsters that can play anywhere, any time, whenever YOU want them to! Ladies and gentlemen...

The Mop Tops!
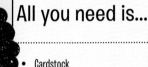

All you need is...

- Cardstock
- Embroidery floss (thread) for hair
- Templates on page 134
- Natural cotton or muslin (calico)
- Fabrics for clothes
- Felt for instruments (optional)

1 Using embroidery floss (thread) and two circles of cardstock, make four pompoms (see page 113). These will form the band's hair.

2 Using the templates on page 134, lightly draw ten finger puppets on natural cotton or muslin (calico). Leave some space between them. One of these will be the band's manager.

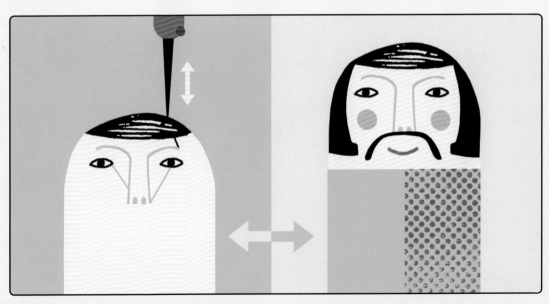

3 Lightly draw features, moustaches, and hair on the front and back templates. Then use the freehand embroidery foot of your sewing machine to sew over your lines.

Match the color of the facial hair to the color of each Mop Top band member's luxuriant hairdo.

4 Referring to the templates on page 134, cut out the band's snazzy stage outfits (and a sharp suit for the manager) from fabric of your choice. The type of fabric you use depends on what sort of band you want to make–psychedelic prints, pin-stripes, spangly satin... Be creative by cutting out shapes or flowers that could be added as details such as collars. Assemble the ensembles for the front and backs of your puppets, secure with fabric glue, and then sew over the top with your embroidery foot.

5 Cut out your band members, without cutting over your stitch lines. Turn under and press a ¼-in. (6-mm) hem at the bottom of each and sew.

6 Pin each front to its corresponding back, right sides together, and sew around the sides, taking a ¼-in. (6-mm) seam and leaving the straight bottom edge open. Turn right side out.

7 No Mop Top would be complete without his/her signature mop top hair-do, so take a needle and matching thread and sew the hair onto the seam at the top of each band member's head. Leave the manager as he is.

Your finger-pickin' friends are ready to take the stage.

It's Mop Top mania!

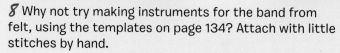

8 Why not try making instruments for the band from felt, using the templates on page 134? Attach with little stitches by hand.

They're a hairy handful and fingers full of fun!

Lend me your ears!

Here are some clever ways to make use of some of the other projects featured in this book, which will have you grinning from ear to ear!

Felt rose earrings

You will need

- Felt
- Earring stud posts
- Glue gun

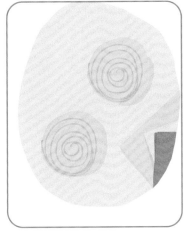

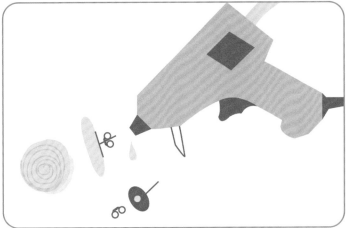

1 Make two felt roses (see page 76), omitting the leaves.

2 Using a glue gun, stick them onto the stud posts.

Felt ball earrings

You will need

- Wool tops
- Earring stud posts
- Glue gun

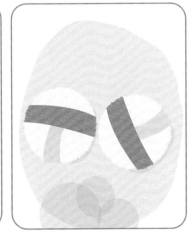

1 Make two felt balls (see pages 66–7), but try mixing in different colors of wool.

2 Using a glue gun, stick them onto the stud posts.

Fabric button earrings

You will need

- Self-cover buttons, approx. ⅜ in. (1 cm) in diameter

- Fabric scraps

- Glue gun

1 Cover two self-cover buttons with fabric (see page 31).

2 Using a glue gun, stick them onto the stud posts.

Strings & Needles

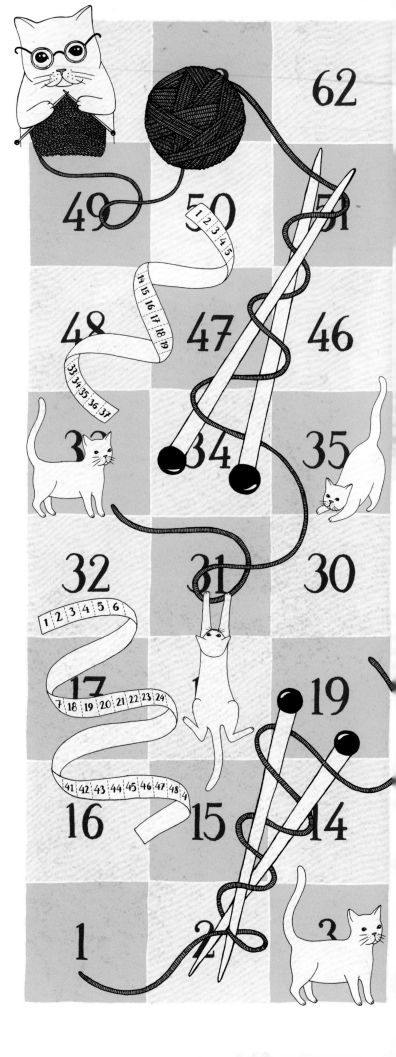

Use a dice and buttons for counters to start your journey at 1. Every time you land on the lower end of a pair of knitting needles, climb up them to the other end. If you land at the top of a tape measure, slide down to the bottom.

The first player to reach granny is the winner!

Come to Light

Thrifty Thelma and Woolly the Lamb upcycle a lampshade

Materials you will need

- Lampshade frame
- Damp cloth
- Fabric strips 1½ in. (4 cm) wide and 5 in. (13 cm) longer than the length of each bar
- Glue gun
- Lots of beads/old necklaces
- Pliers
- Ribbons
- Beading wire
- Masking tape
- Embroidery floss (thread)
- Gathered lace trim
- Buttons
- Felt flower embellishments

1 Thrifty Thelma and Woolly the Lamb are stripping the ugly fabric from their lampshade. They want to give it a fresh new look. Once all the fabric has been taken off, they clean it with a damp cloth.

2 They tear strips of fabric to wrap around each bar. Then they add glue to the top of the bar with a glue gun, wrap the strip of fabric round tightly all the way down to the bottom, and secure it with another dab of glue. They do this to every vertical bar. And because they tore the fabric, the strips are frayed, which Thelma and Woolly like.

3 Next, Thelma measures around the inner circular section where the light bulb goes. She finds an old necklace that she never wears, cuts it to size using pliers, and then attaches it to the frame using a glue gun.

4 For each of the sections between the vertical bars, they cut two ribbons about 1½ in. (4 cm) longer than the bars. Then they sew two or three felt flowers onto each one. They wrap the tops of the ribbons to the top of the frame, securing with glue, and do the same to the bottom.

5 They thread beads onto beading wire the same length as the ribbons and stick masking tape to the ends, so that the beads don't fall off. Then they tie the wires to the top and bottom of the frame, in between the ribbons, adding a dab of glue to each knot for extra security. They also attach some old bead necklaces.

6 Thelma and Woolly cut lengths of embroidery floss in different colors and wrap them around the top and bottom of the frame, all the way around.

7 They glue another beaded necklace along the top of the lampshade. Then they measure their gathered lace to the circumference of the frame base and attach it with glue. To finish it off, they glue buttons onto the lace at the bottom of each bar and add a few more felt flowers to the bar frames for luck.

Odsey *makes a* pillow

Let's see what Odsey is up to… she's got all her sewing stuff out and she's making a soft felt pillow! This girl wants to relax in style.

Materials you will need

- Felt
- Templates on page 116
- Four self-cover buttons

- Fabric for buttons
- Two buttons for the pillow back
- Pillow form (cushion pad)

- Ruler
- Automatic buttonhole foot
- Un-picker

1 First, she measures her pillow (cushion) and divides it into four squares. From felt she cuts out four squares of different colors, adding ³⁄₈ in. (1 cm) all around each piece to allow for the seams.

2 Using the templates on page 116, she cuts out petal shapes from felt—16 big and 16 small (you can re-size them to fit).

3 She draws a criss-cross from corner to corner on each square, glues a line along the center of each big petal, and sticks four petals onto each square to form a flower shape growing out from the center point.

4 Then she glues the smaller petals on top of the larger ones, radiating from the same center point. With her sewing machine, she sews a criss-cross through the center of her petals to the corners of each square.

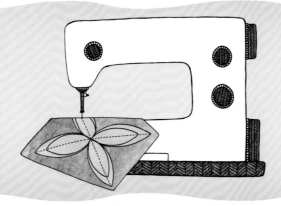

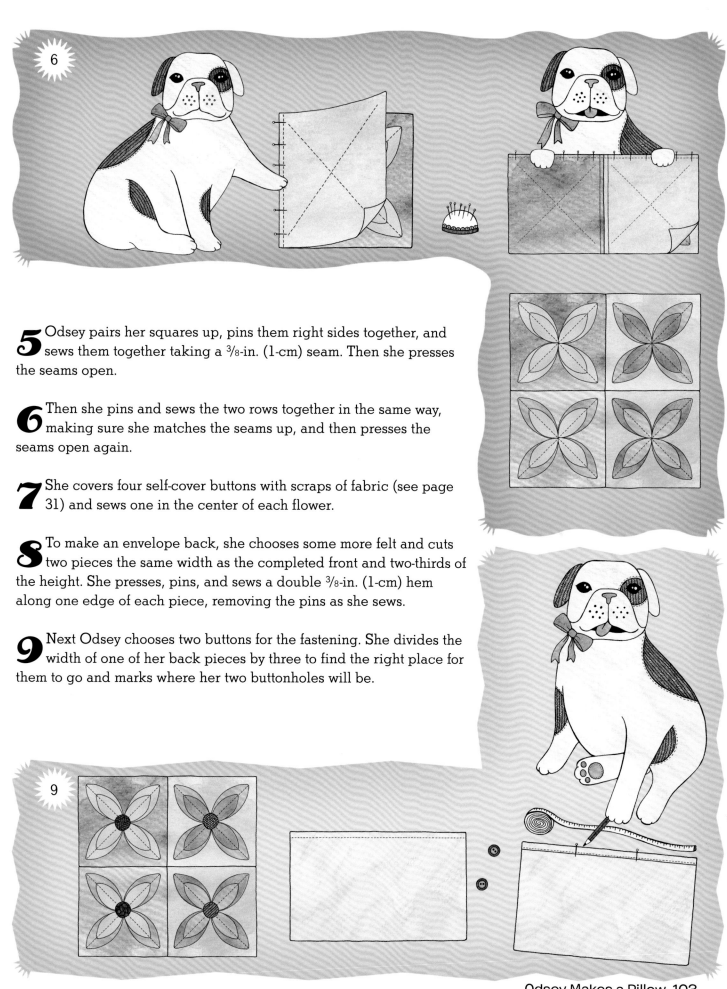

5 Odsey pairs her squares up, pins them right sides together, and sews them together taking a 3/8-in. (1-cm) seam. Then she presses the seams open.

6 Then she pins and sews the two rows together in the same way, making sure she matches the seams up, and then presses the seams open again.

7 She covers four self-cover buttons with scraps of fabric (see page 31) and sews one in the center of each flower.

8 To make an envelope back, she chooses some more felt and cuts two pieces the same width as the completed front and two-thirds of the height. She presses, pins, and sews a double 3/8-in. (1-cm) hem along one edge of each piece, removing the pins as she sews.

9 Next Odsey chooses two buttons for the fastening. She divides the width of one of her back pieces by three to find the right place for them to go and marks where her two buttonholes will be.

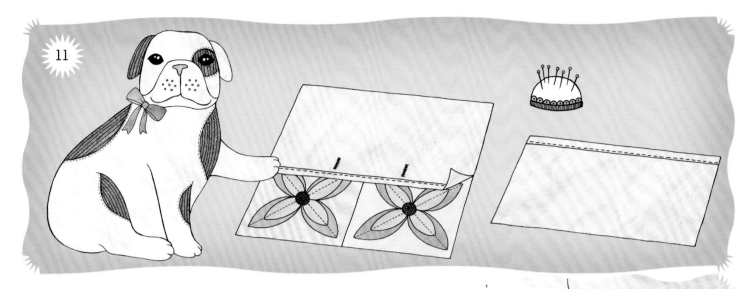

10 She uses her automatic buttonhole foot to sew the buttonholes, but you can also do this manually by pivoting a standard buttonhole foot (see page 112). She opens the buttonholes with an un-picker.

11 She lays the front of the pillow down, right side facing up. Then she lays the back piece with the buttonholes across the top of this, right side facing down, and the bottom half over this, again facing down.

12 She pins them together and sews all the way around, taking a ³⁄₈-in. (1-cm) seam.

13 Odsey trims all the seam allowances and turns the cover right side out. She marks through the buttonholes where the buttons should go, and sews them on, then inserts a pillow form (cushion pad).

14 Finally she fluffs up the petals, lays her head on her new comfy pillow... and falls fast asleep. Sweet dreams, Odsey!

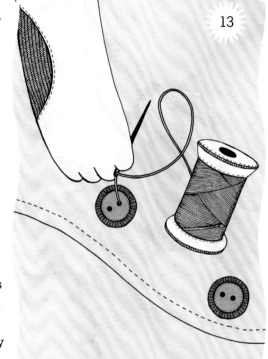

Bertie Badger
smartens up a suitcase

Bertie Badger is going off on his travels. He hums a tune as he packs his suitcase. Camera, bucket and spade, teabags... hold on a minute! He pauses and looks at his suitcase. It's very old. "This just won't do," he says, and he takes everything out again. He'll come back to this later... there are more pressing matters at hand.

Materials you will need

- A suitcase
- Lots of fabric
- Mod Podge glue (matt or gloss)
- Paintbrush
- Rotary cutter (optional)

1 He collects a big bundle of fabric and starts cutting out shapes–flowers, patterns, whatever catches his eye–until he has a nice big pile to work with.

2 After giving it a wipe with a damp cloth to clean it, he brushes some glue directly onto a small area of the suitcase and starts sticking his scraps of fabric on top. He then brushes more glue on top of his fabric, smoothing out any wrinkles and bubbles as he goes.

3 He repeats the process, layering it on gradually in small areas. He takes his time when he reaches the edges, handles, and catches, trimming the fabric carefully with scissors (you could also use a rotary cutter), and folding it over to the inside of the suitcase.

4 When the suitcase is completely covered in fabric, he brushes glue all over the fabric to seal it and leaves it to dry for a few hours. Now he can get on with his packing.

***Bon voyage*, Bertie!**

Throw for

This is a game for two or more players. Each player gets four shots.

Take turns to throw buttons onto these colorful characters, see where they land, and tot up your scores to find the winner!

Points!

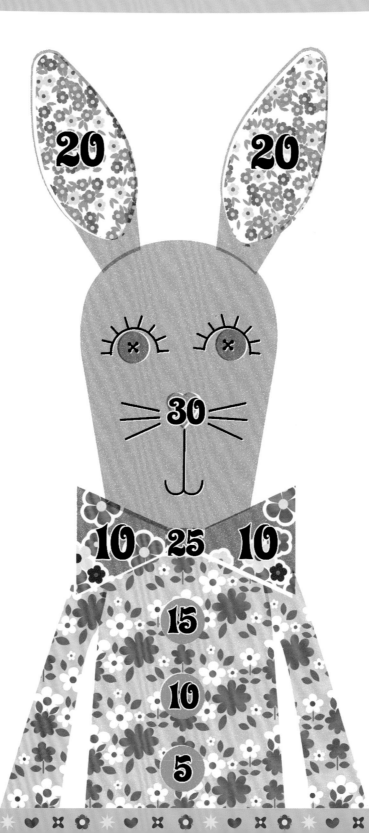

Techniques

The techniques used in this book are nice and simple, though if you haven't come across a particular one before, practice on some scrap fabric before you start your project.

Preparing fabric

If you are recycling fabric from old clothes or soft furnishings, launder it to make sure it's nice and fresh. You can cut around permanent stains, but if the item is a bit smelly, then your project will smell, too!

If you are using multiple fabrics and the finished project will need laundering at some point in its life, then do make sure that the fabrics you're using can be washed together and that colors won't run. You can test for color-fastness by dipping a bit of the fabric in warm water and then squeezing it with white kitchen paper.

If the fabric is creased, give it a quick press before you use it; it's always easier to work on smooth, crisp fabric.

Using templates

All the templates you'll need are on pages 115–142. Most are full size, so all you need to do is photocopy them and cut them out. The templates for the Pinboard (page 86) can be enlarged or reduced to suit the size of your frame. Sometimes you'll need to flip a template to produce a front and back; the projects will tell you when to do this. For outlines, just cut out the template and draw around it with a vanishinf fabric marker pen. To transfer details within the template onto fabric, you can tape the template to a window with masking tape, then tape the fabric over it. You should be able to trace off the detail onto the fabric. But do feel free to draw your own details, just using the template as reference.

Attaching motifs before sewing

If the motifs are quite big, you can pin them onto the background fabric before sewing them in place. However, if there are lots of small pieces, it will be easiest to glue them on. Use proper fabric glue and just little dabs of it in the middle of each piece; try not to use lots of glue or it'll stain the fabric and make it gloopy and difficult to sew. Alternatively, you can baste (tack) pieces in place with hand stitches in a contrast color thread (to make them easy to see and take out later).

You can also use fusible webbing to hold pieces in place. This is a heat-sensitive film on a paper backing that you iron onto the wrong side of the fabric. You then draw the shape you want on the paper backing, cut it out, peel the backing off, and iron the shape onto the background. You can buy a special sew-able webbing that won't clog up your machine needle as much. Always follow the manufacturer's instructions when using fusible webbing to avoid mistakes.

Fusible interfacing

This is interfacing with a heat-sensitive film on one side. If you are using thin fabric, you just iron it onto the wrong side of your fabric to stiffen and strengthen it. It's always a good idea to test a bit of interfacing on a scrap of the fabric first, as it can pucker permanently.

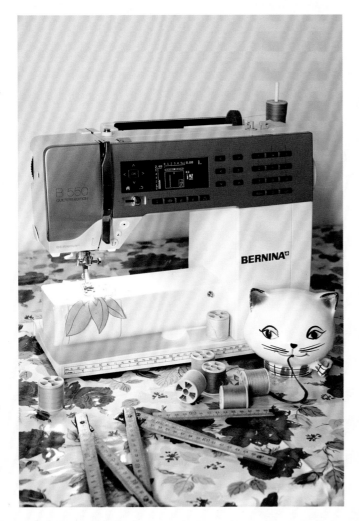

Using a sewing machine

You don't need to be very skilled with a sewing machine to make projects in this book, but if you've not used one very often, or it's a while since you last stitched, then spend some time polishing up on your skills by sewing bits of scrap fabric to get used to it. As well as ordinary straight stitching, there is a lot of machine embroidery in many of the projects, so you will need a freehand machine embroidery foot (see page 112) for your sewing machine if you haven't got one. Other than that, you only need a straight foot and a zig-zag foot.

It's always a good idea to read the sewing-machine instruction manual again to make sure you're threading and using the machine properly.

The stitch you'll use most will be a medium-length straight stitch, so test that out. Also experiment with any zig-zag and decorative stitches your machine might have and, if appropriate, make a note of the machine settings that work best with each one.

The most important thing to get right is the tension. There'll be a dial on the front of your machine that you turn to adjust the spool tension; the larger the number, the tighter the tension.

Here, the top tension is too loose and the top thread is being pulled through to the bobbin side of the seam.

Here, the top tension is too tight and the bobbin thread is being pulled to the top.

This diagram shows balanced tension, with the top and bobbin threads interlocking within the layers of fabric.

Sewing seams

Before you start each project, sew a seam on a scrap bit of the project fabric to check that your tension is right. On the throat plate (the metal plate under the needle) of the machine, there will be marks showing different widths of seam allowance. Just pick the width you need and line up the raw edge of the fabric with the mark. Sew quite slowly, keeping the edge of the fabric on the mark, and your seam or hem will be neat and accurate.

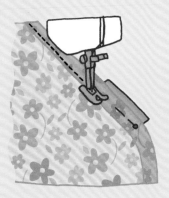

Topstitching

I use this technique in some projects and if you've not done it before it's definitely one you should practice. You sew a line of straight stitch very close to the edge of the project; about ⅛ in. (2 mm) in from the edge is good. The trick is to position the fabric under the needle and lower the needle into the fabric to check it'll be sewing in the right place. Then, if there isn't a mark on the throat plate in the right place, stick a piece of masking tape to the plate at the edge of the fabric. Keep the edge of the fabric against the tape as you sew and your topstitching will look great.

Freehand machine embroidery

I think this is the nicest way of using a sewing machine. "Draw" details onto the project with the needle and "color in" areas. Go over stitching several times to give a sketchy, scribbled look; it doesn't have to be neat to look great.

This is another technique you'll want to practice if you're not familiar with it. The best thing to do is to experiment on a piece of scrap fabric until you feel confident; this gives you the opportunity to adjust the tension, too.

Your sewing machine will have feed dogs that come up into the throat plate as you sew and pull the fabric through. To embroider you need to drop the feed dogs; your sewing machine manual will tell you how to do it on your particular machine. Once the dogs are down you can move the fabric in any direction under the needle, as fast or as slow as you wish.

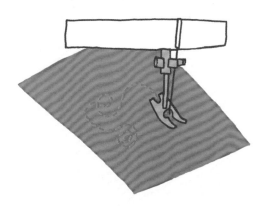

You'll need a freehand machine embroidery foot, sometimes called a darning foot or a free-motion foot. This stops the fabric from lifting while you sew. You might find it helpful to fit the fabric into an embroidery hoop while you sew, to keep it flat and taut and prevent any puckering. You can buy special easy-to-use hoops for machine embroidery, or use a traditional wooden one—it'll work just as well.

Once you're ready, set the stitch length on the machine to zero, and off you go. Start slowly to get the feel of the stitching and see how fast you need to move the fabric to achieve the look you want. Think of the fabric as a piece of paper and the needle as a pencil and reverse it in your brain so you're moving the paper to make the design.

Be VERY careful to keep your fingers away from the needle as you move the fabric about under it.

Trimming corners

If you've seamed a corner, you need to clip off excess fabric before you turn the project right side out to ensure that the finished corner is neat and square. Cut off the fabric across the corner as shown, cutting about ⅛ in. (2 mm) away from the line of stitching.

Notching curves

Curved seams need notches cutting out of the seam allowances so that, when the project is turned right side out, the seam allowances lie flat and the seam isn't puckered. Cut small notches with the tips of the scissors to about ⅛ in. (2mm) away from the line of stitching. Space the notches about ¾ in. (2 cm) apart on the curves.

Making buttonholes

If you have an automatic buttonhole feature on your sewing machine, use that and a buttonhole foot to sew the buttonholes. To sew buttonholes manually, set your machine to a narrow zigzag. Sew down the left side of the marked buttonhole. Lift the presser foot and pivot the fabric 180 degrees. Lower the presser foot and double the stitch width. Hold the fabric firmly, so that it doesn't slip, and let the machine make a few side-to-side stitches. Return the stitch width to its prior setting and sew up the other side of the buttonhole, then make a few longer stitches, as before. Using your seam unpicker, cut through the fabric to open the buttonholes, being careful not to cut the threads.

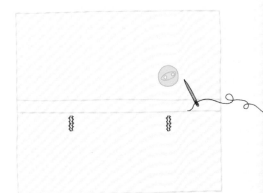

Making a pom-pom

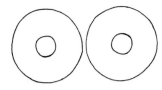

1 Cut out two circles of card the size you want the pom-pom to be. Cut a smaller circle out of the middle of each, so they look like rings.

2 Place the rings on top of each other and, using manageable lengths, wind knitting yarn around the rings, using an embroidery needle if it makes it easier. Feed the yarn through the circle in the middle and wind it around the card. If you come to the end of a length of yarn, there's no need to tie the ends; just make sure that the end is on the outside of the ring rather than the inside. Continue this until all the card is covered and the hole is nearly full of wound yarn.

3 Now cut the yarn around the outside of the rings, a little bit at a time.

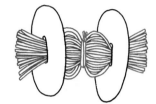

4 Thread another piece of yarn between the card rings and tie it tightly–very tightly– around the bunched strands of yarn.

5 Remove the cardboard rings–you might need to cut them off. Trim any unruly ends of yarn.

Types of stitch

Backstitch

Bring the needle through the fabric and take a short backward stitch on the stitching line. Bring the needle through a stitch-length in front of the first stitch. Take the needle down where it first came through and repeat to sew the seam.

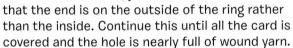

Blanket stitch

From the front, make a stitch through the fabric, coming out on the stitching line. Loop the working thread under the point of the needle. Pull the needle through and tighten the stitch. Continue in this way, spacing the stitches evenly for a neat finish. To avoid distorting stitches or puckering fabric, tighten the thread gently.

Running stitch

Make a series of small stitches along the stitching line. They can be of even lengths and equally spaced, or more random, whichever you prefer the look of.

Slip stitch

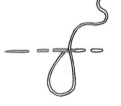

This is used to close gaps in seams. Bring the needle up through one piece of fabric at the start of the gap. Take it across to the other piece and make a tiny stitch through that. Pull the stitch tight, but not so tight that the fabric puckers. Take the needle across to the other piece and make the next tiny stitch. Continue in this way to sew up the whole gap.

Straight stitch

Make a small straight stitch where needed. Repeat as required!

Crafty Supplies

For vintage fabrics:

Donna Flower
www.donnaflower.com

Pommedejour
www.pommedejour.com

I'm very grateful to you both for your gorgeous vintage fabrics and wallpapers used throughout this book, and for keeping my fabric addiction alive!

For new fabrics:

Amy Butler
www.amybutlerdesign.com

Sis Boom
www.sisboom.com

Alexander Henry fabrics
www.ahfabrics.com

Thank you all for supplying me with your stunning fabrics!

Upholstery Queen–Daveen
www.daveenchi.com
Thank you for a lovely day and for sharing skills together.

US Suppliers

Heather Bailey
www.heatherbaileystore.com

Free Spirit
www.freespiritfabric.com

Hobby Lobby
www.hobbylobby.com

Joann Fabric & Craft Stores
www.joann.com

Michael Miller Fabrics
www.michaelmillerfabrics.com

Michaels
www.michaels.com

Reprodepot Fabrics
www.reprodepotfabrics.com

Westminster Fibers
www.westminsterfibers.com

UK Suppliers

Fabric Rehab
www.fabricrehab.co.uk

Hobbycraft
www.hobbycraft.co.uk

John Lewis
www.johnlewis.com

Liberty
www.liberty.co.uk

My Fabric House
www.myfabrichouse.co.uk

Seamstar
www.seamstar.co.uk

VV Rouleaux
www.vvrouleaux.com

Templates

All the templates in this section are full size except for the Pinboard templates on page 133, which you can reduce or enlarge to fit your board. Larger pieces have been split in two to fit on the page—you will need to photocopy or trace and cut out both pieces and join them along the short dotted lines marked to make one piece.

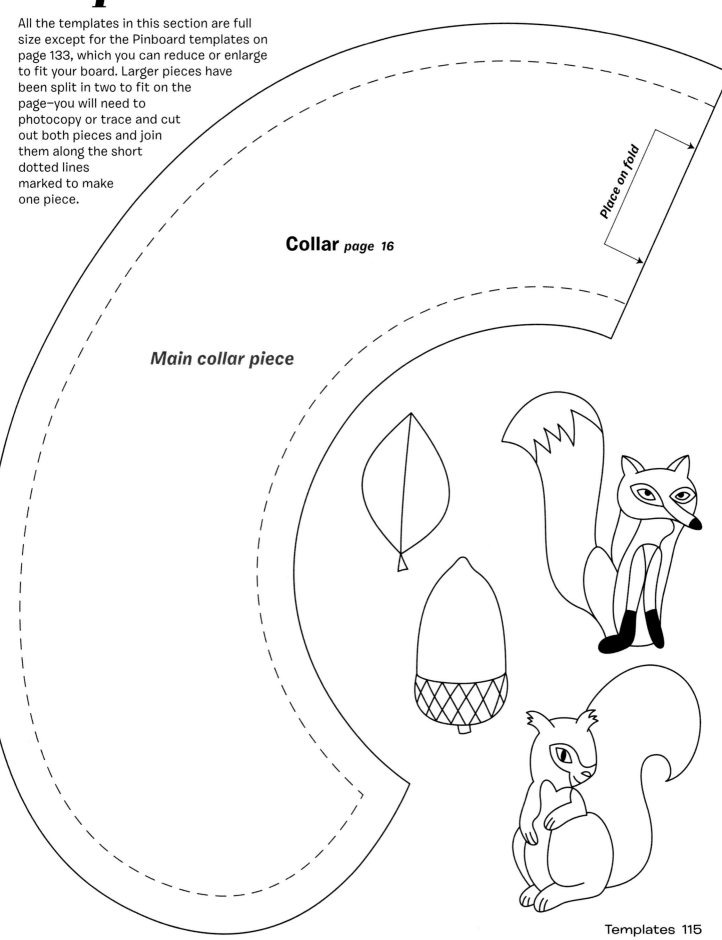

Place on fold

Collar *page 16*

Main collar piece

Jammie Dodger

page 32

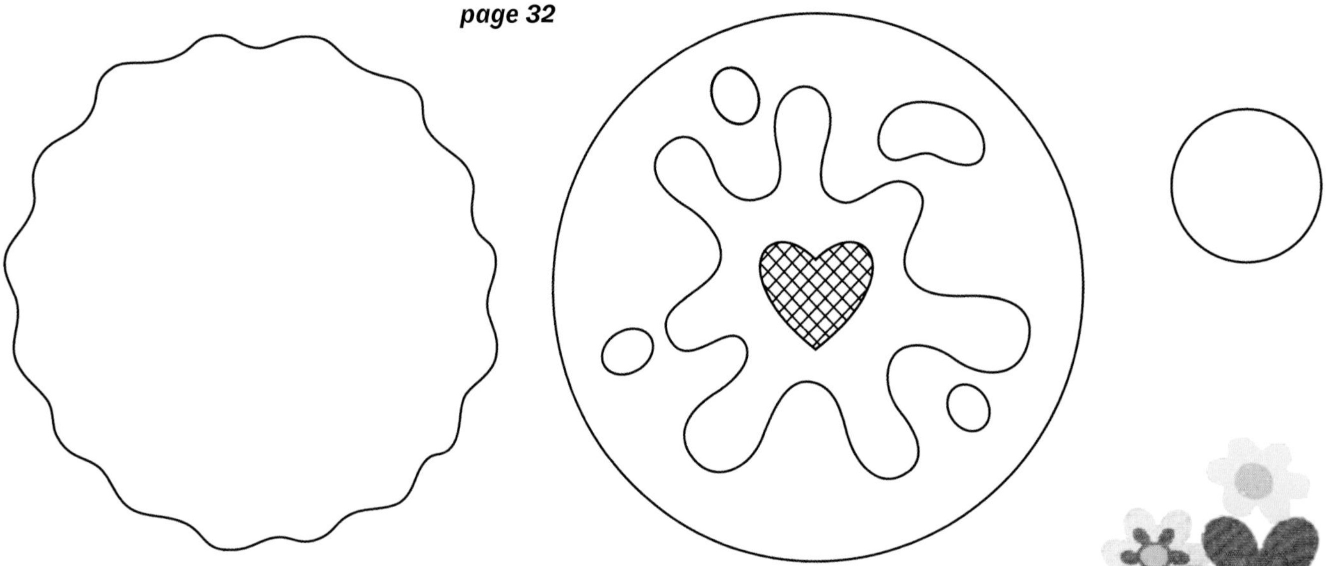

Pillow

page 102

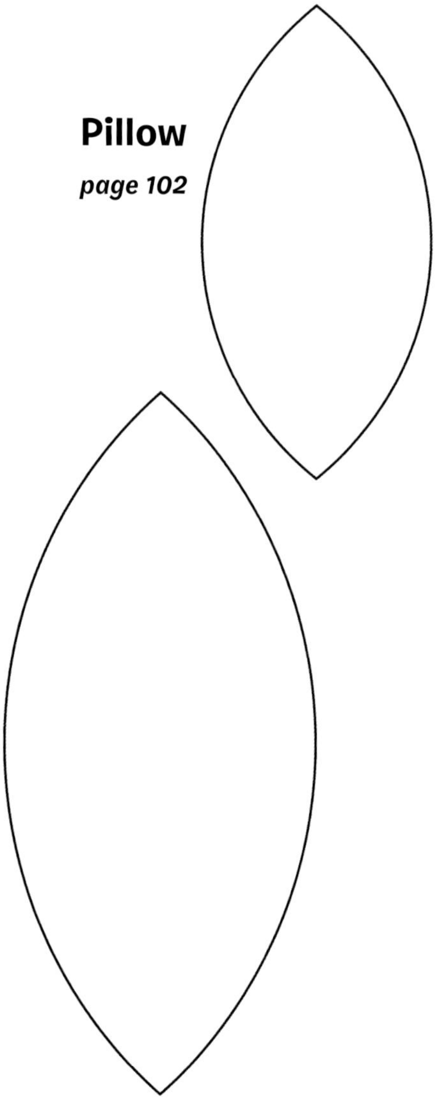

Foxy Lady

page 80

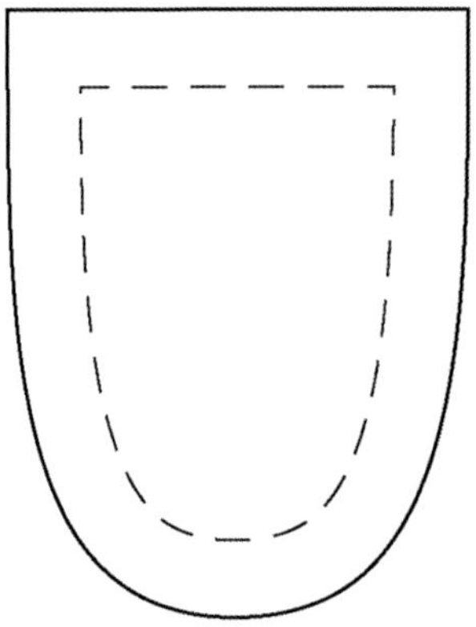

Fox foot

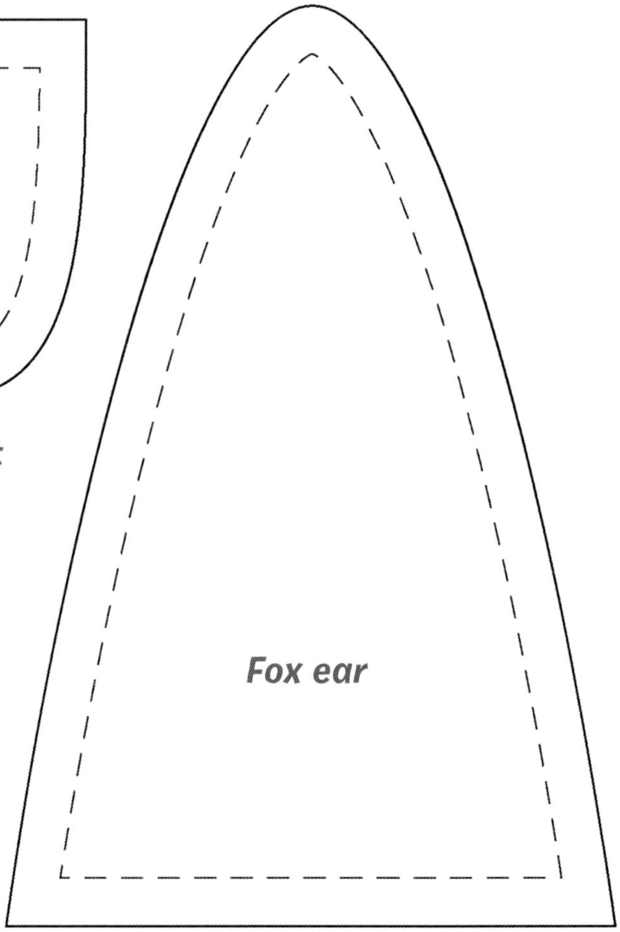

Fox ear

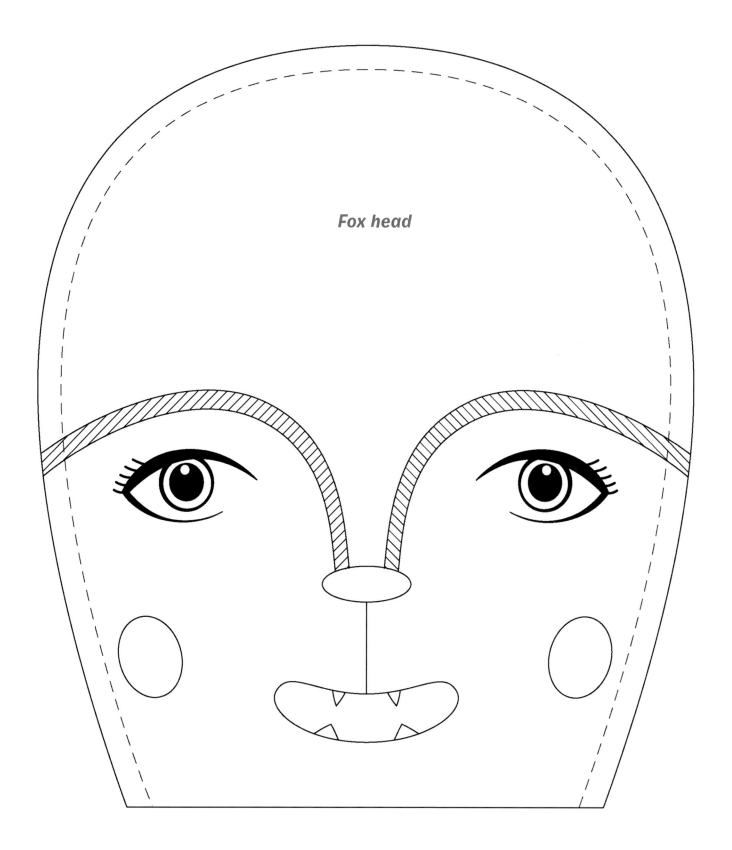

Fox head

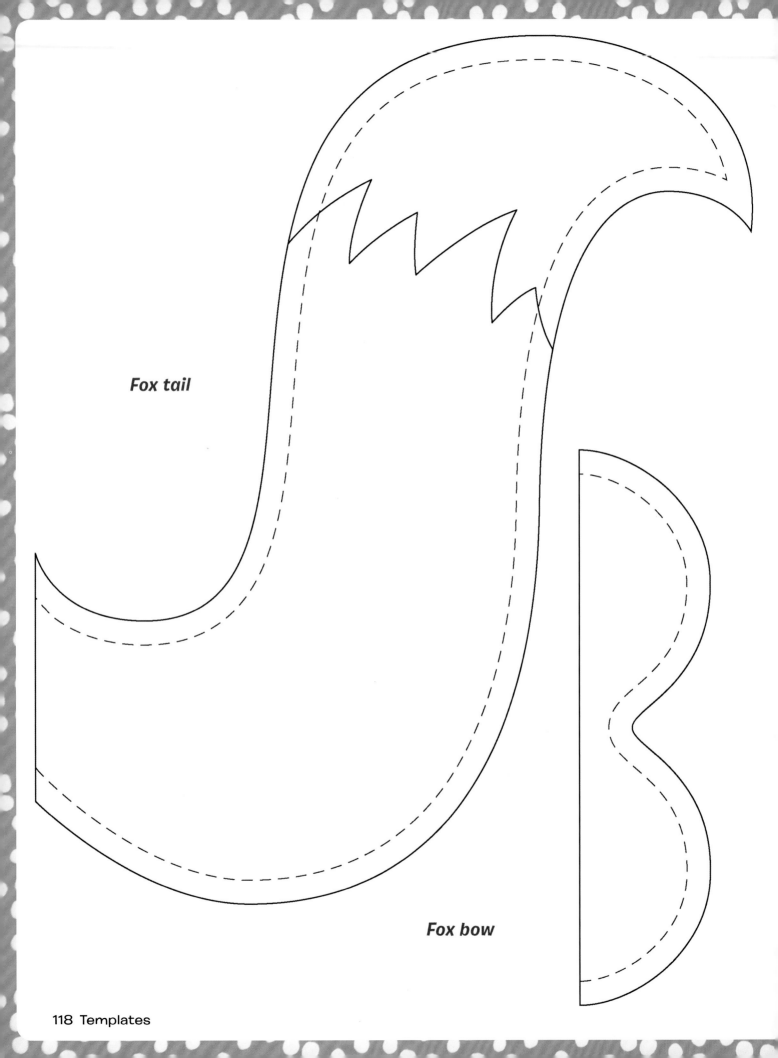

Fox tail

Fox bow

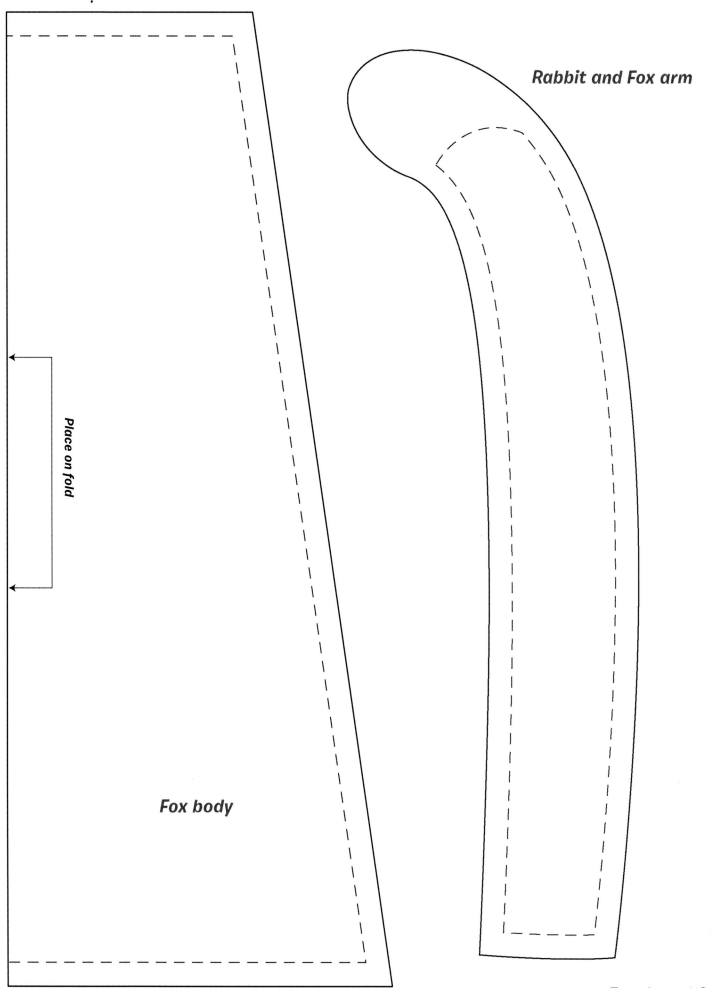

Place on fold

Fox body

Rabbit and Fox arm

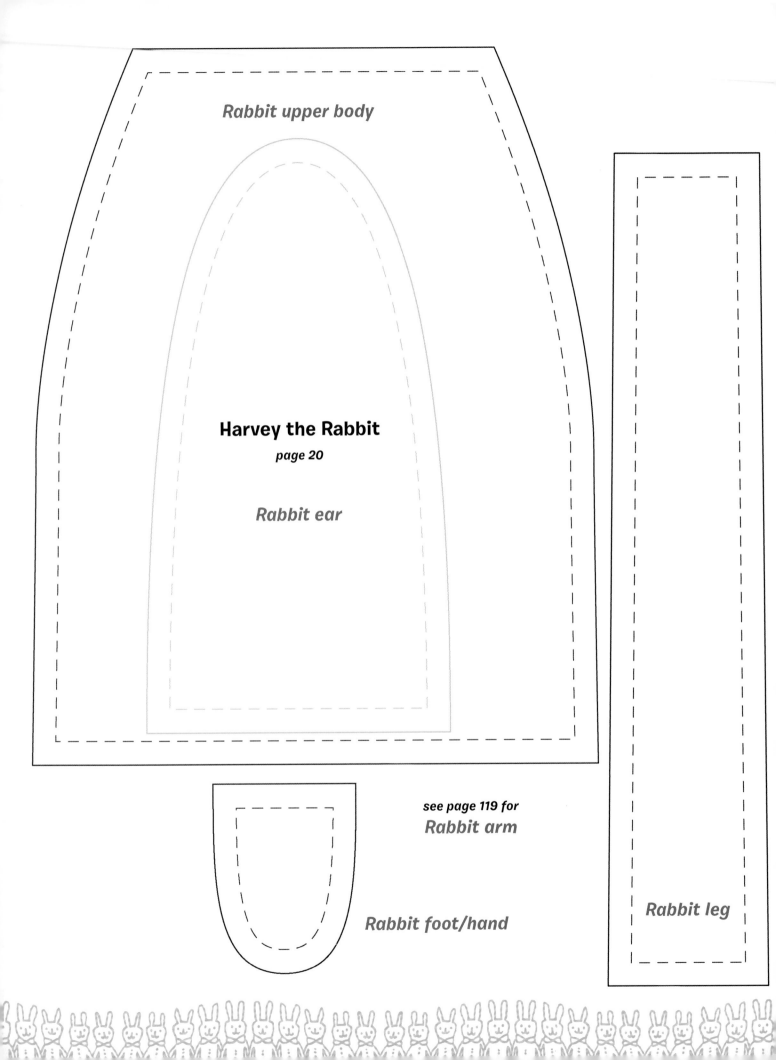

Rabbit upper body

Harvey the Rabbit

page 20

Rabbit ear

see page 119 for
Rabbit arm

Rabbit foot/hand

Rabbit leg

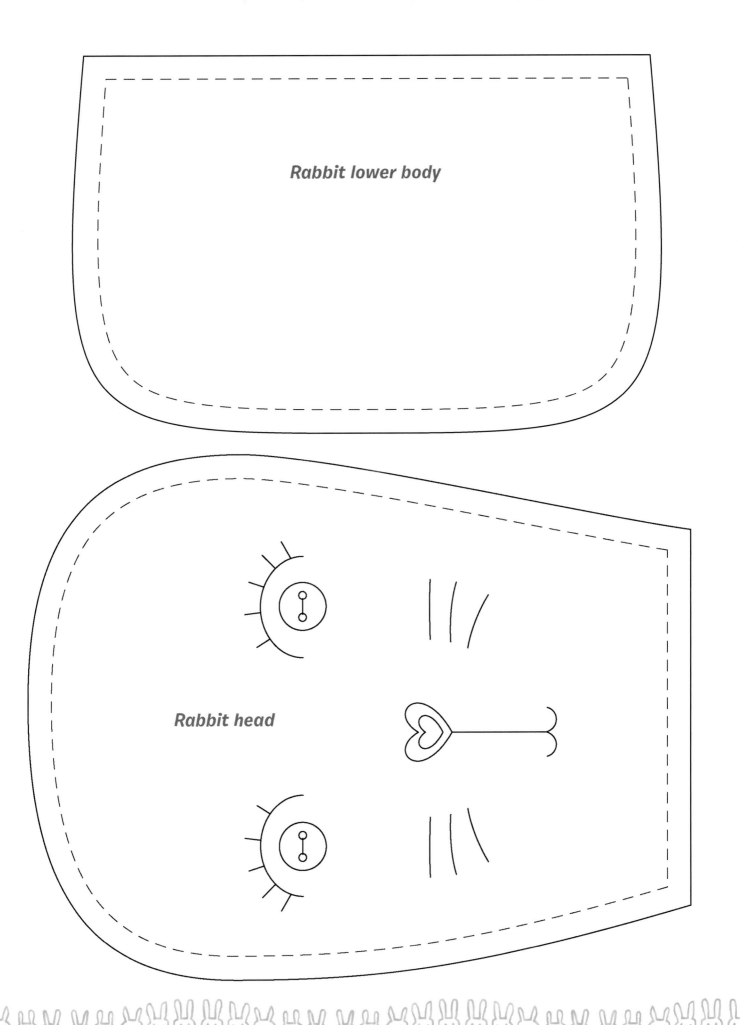

Rabbit lower body

Rabbit head

Clock

page 74

Sink Curtain

page 68

Sink curtain

page 68

Beard

page 44

Place ends of elastic on the white spaces marked

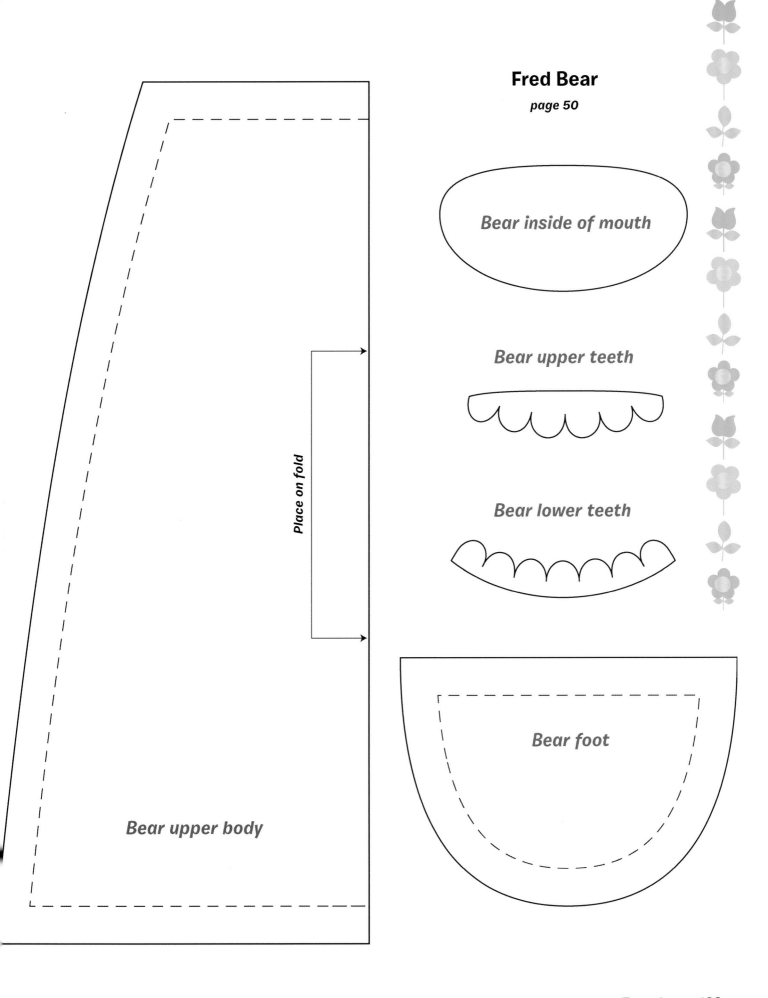

Fred Bear

page 50

Bear inside of mouth

Bear upper teeth

Bear lower teeth

Place on fold

Bear upper body

Bear foot

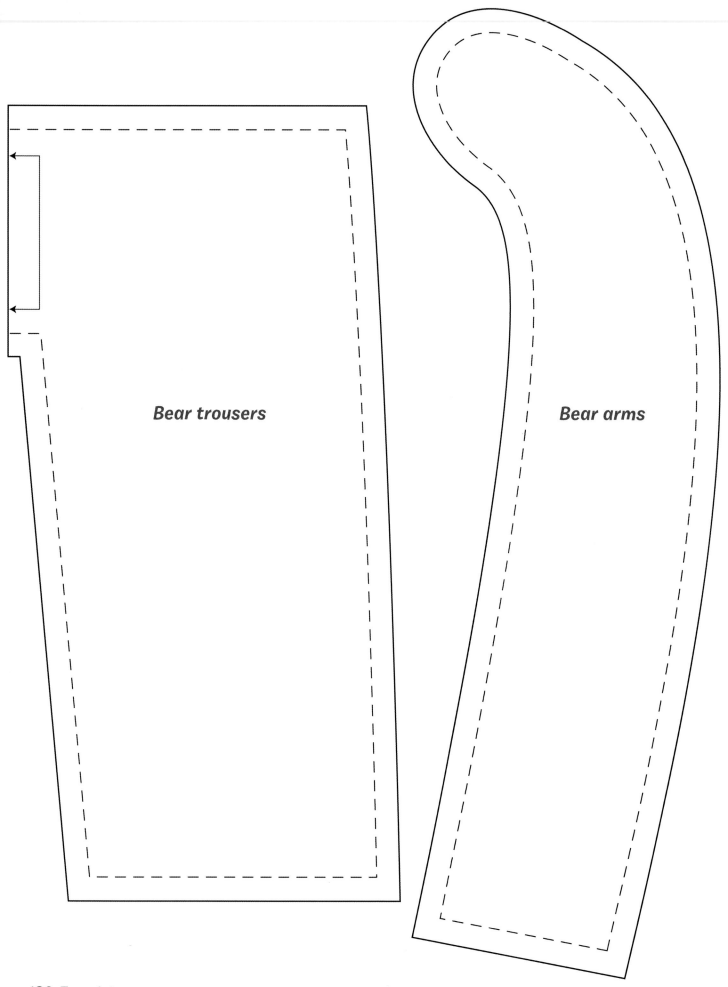

Bear trousers

Bear arms

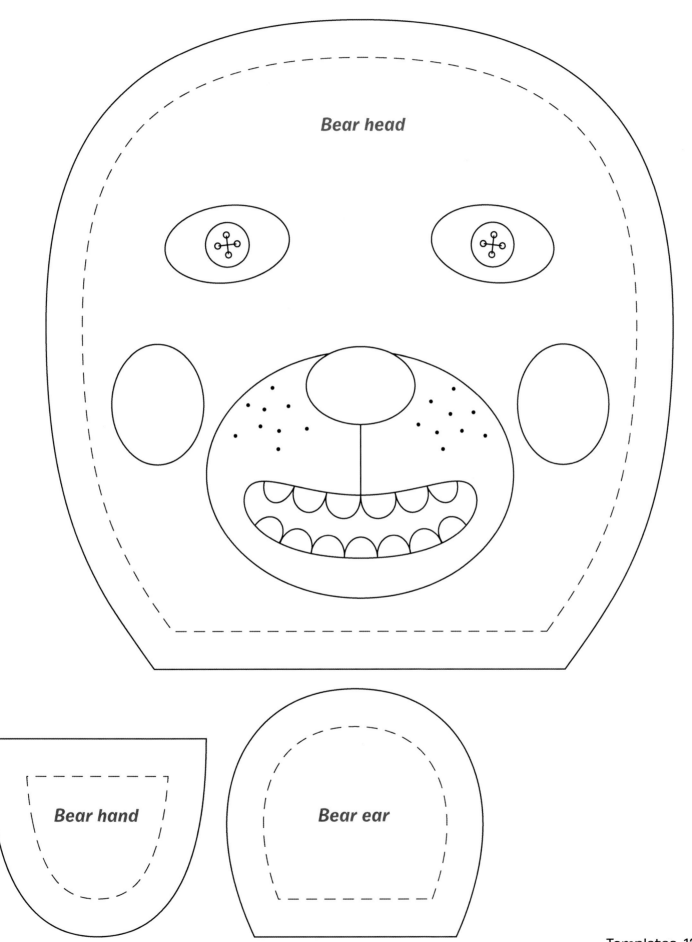

Bear head

Bear hand

Bear ear

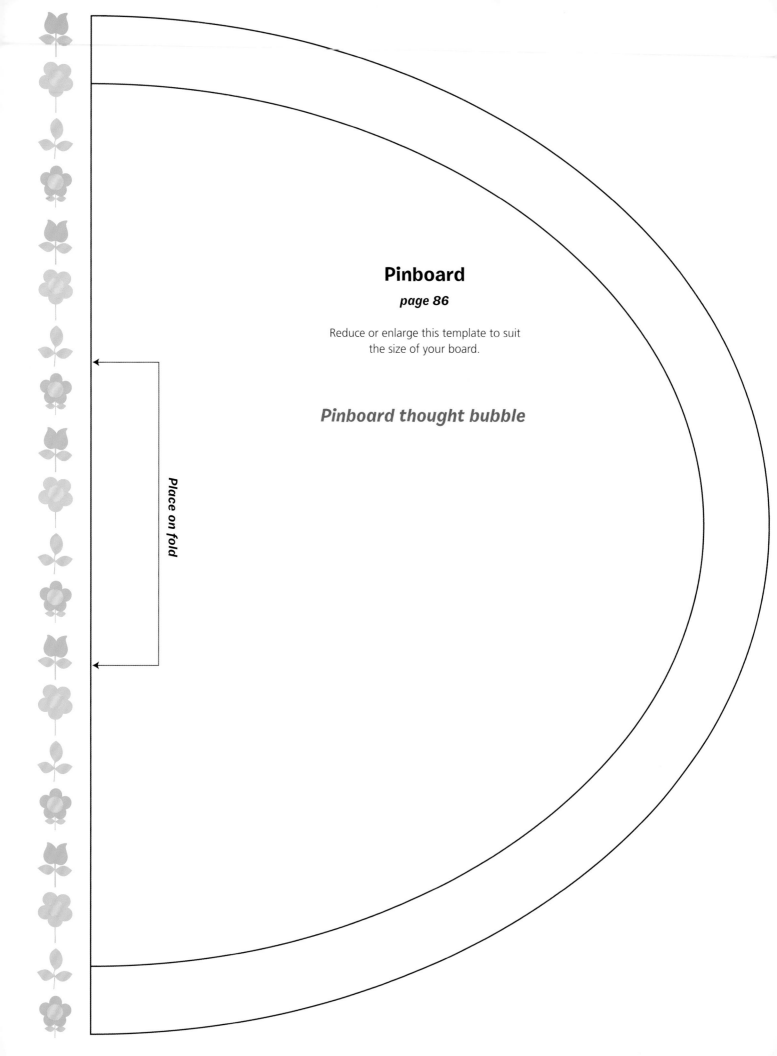

Pinboard

page 86

Reduce or enlarge this template to suit
the size of your board.

Pinboard thought bubble

Place on fold

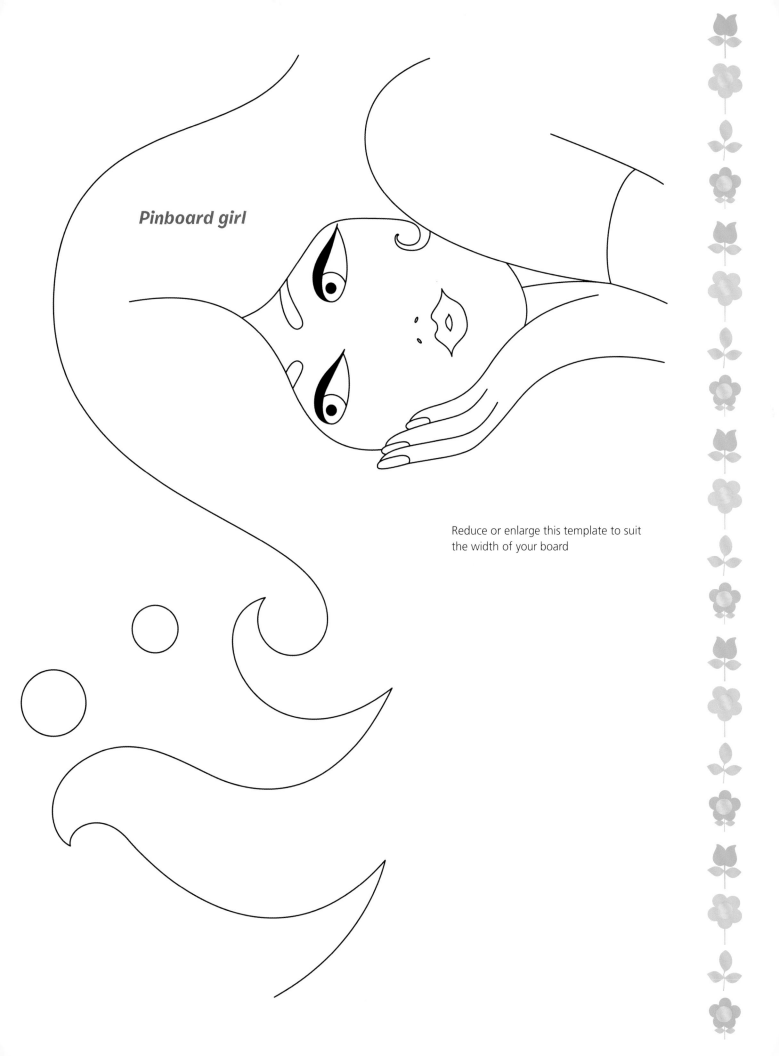

Pinboard girl

Reduce or enlarge this template to suit
the width of your board

Mop Top Puppets

page 92

Funny Face Egg Warmers

page 24

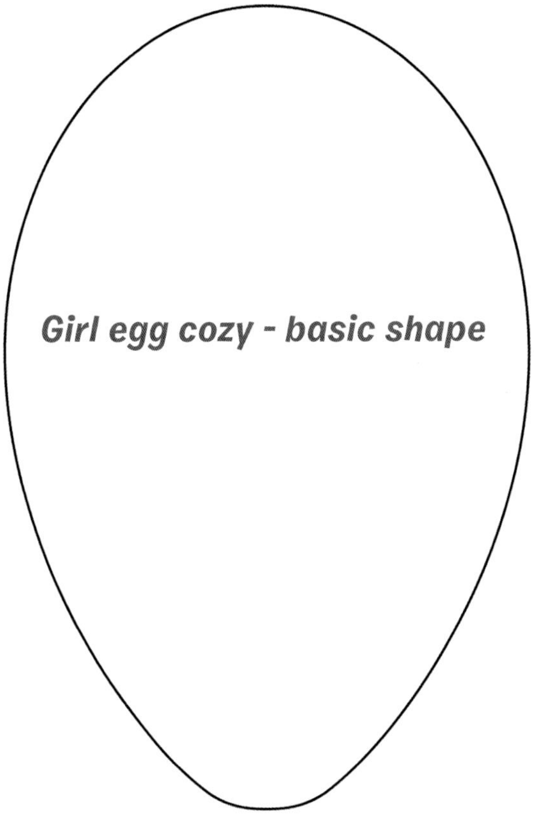

Girl egg cozy - basic shape

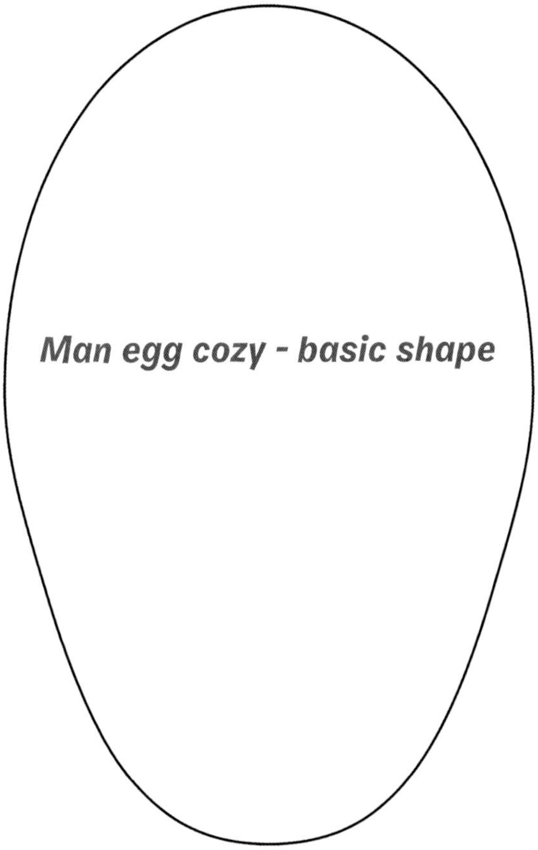

Man egg cozy - basic shape

Girl with blonde hair

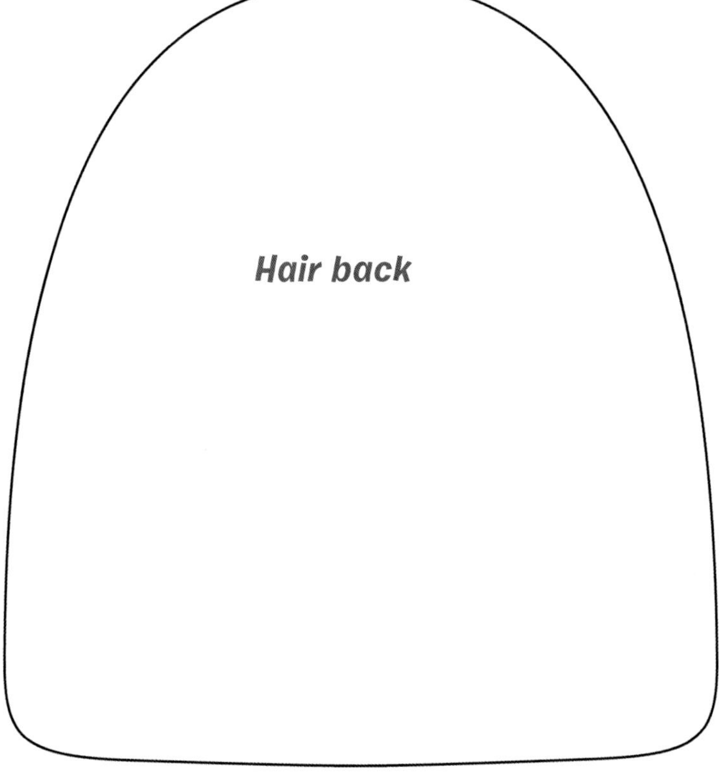

Hair back

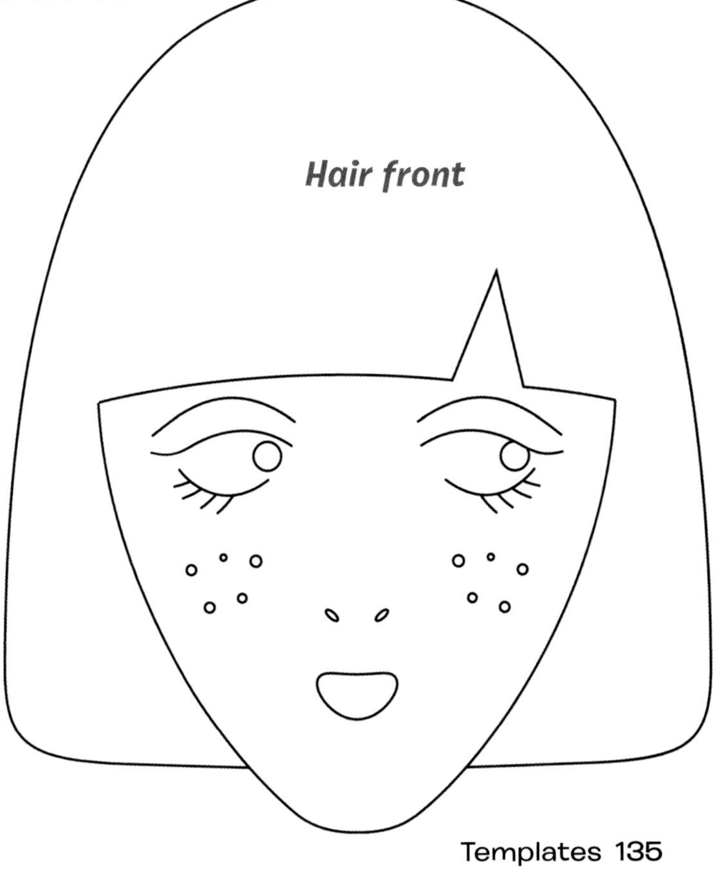

Hair front

Funny Face Egg Warmers
page 24

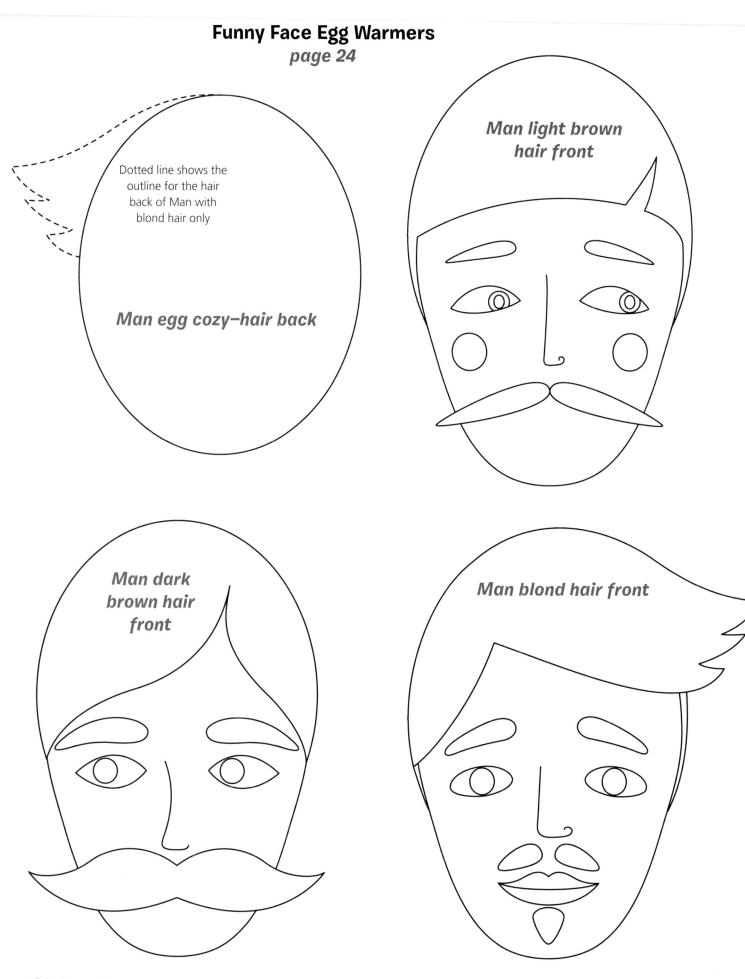

Dotted line shows the outline for the hair back of Man with blond hair only

Man egg cozy–hair back

Man light brown hair front

Man dark brown hair front

Man blond hair front

Girl with red hair

Hair front

Hair back

Girl with orange hair

Hair front

Hair back

Bag

page 46

Join top and bottom pieces of Bag main piece
template along short dotted lines as marked

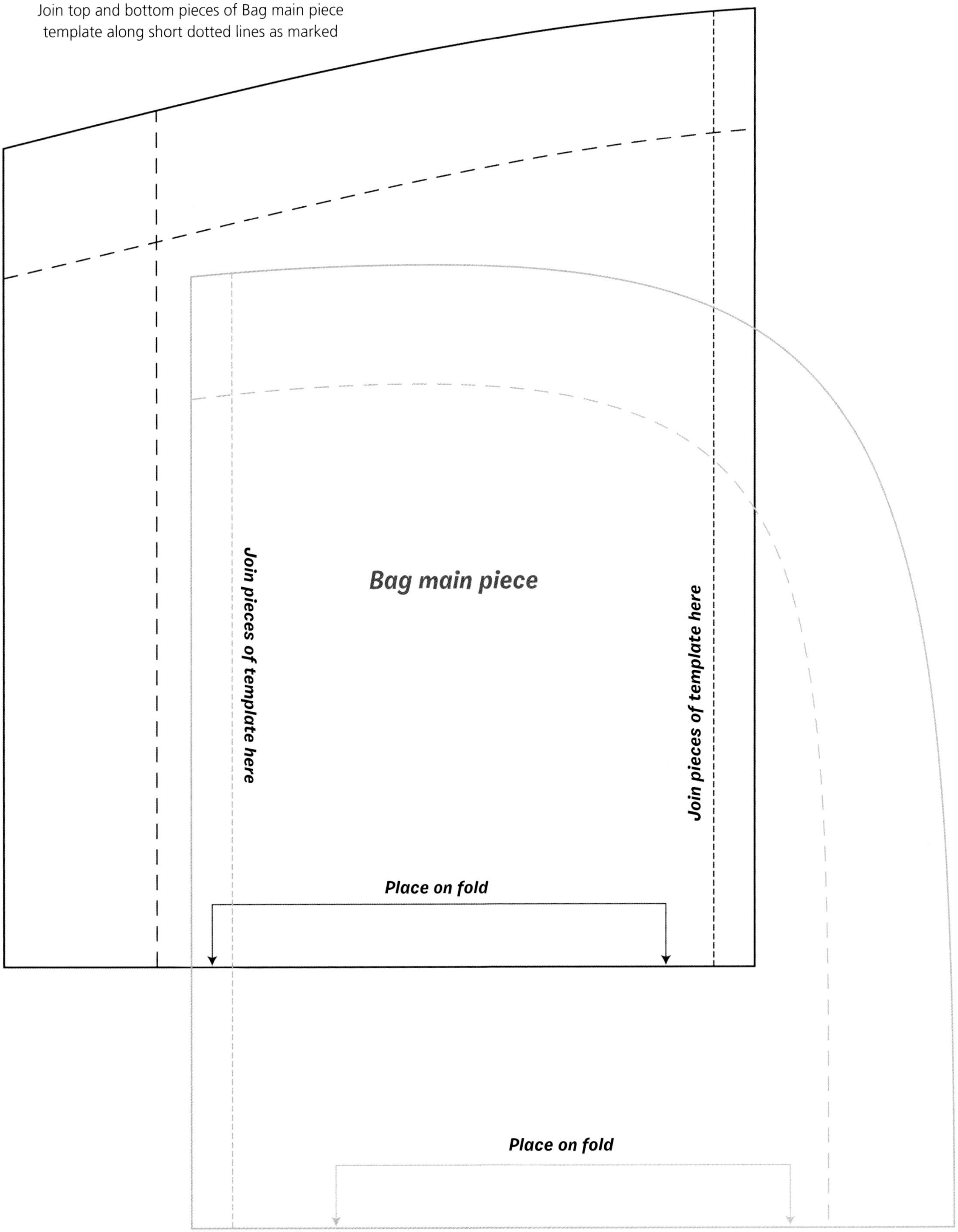

Join pieces of template here

Bag main piece

Join pieces of template here

Place on fold

Place on fold

Headddress

page 36

Place on fold

Bag pocket

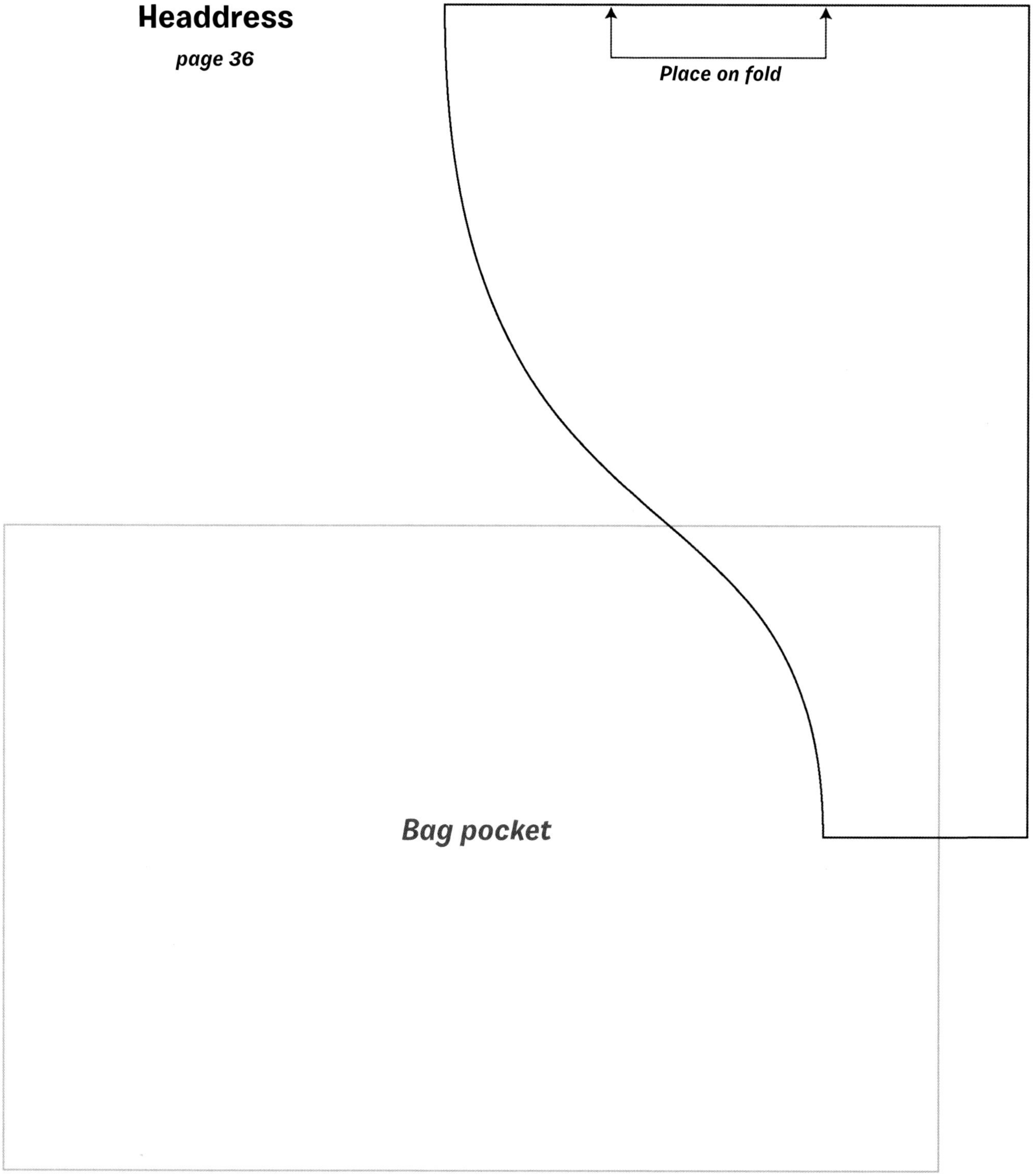

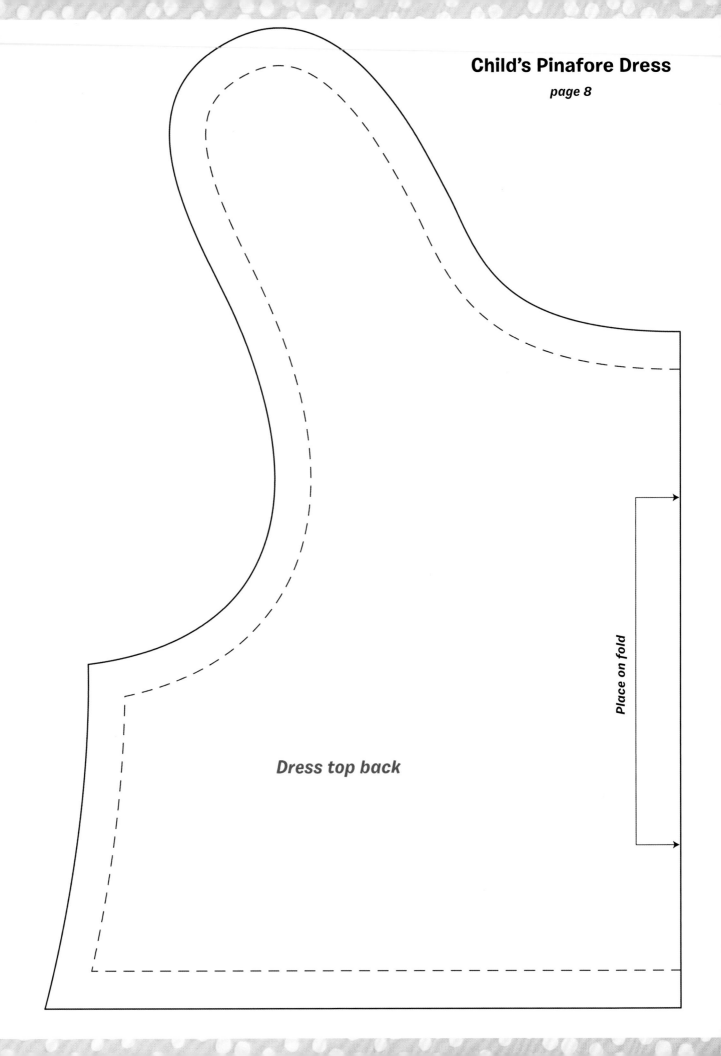

Child's Pinafore Dress

page 8

Place on fold

Dress top back

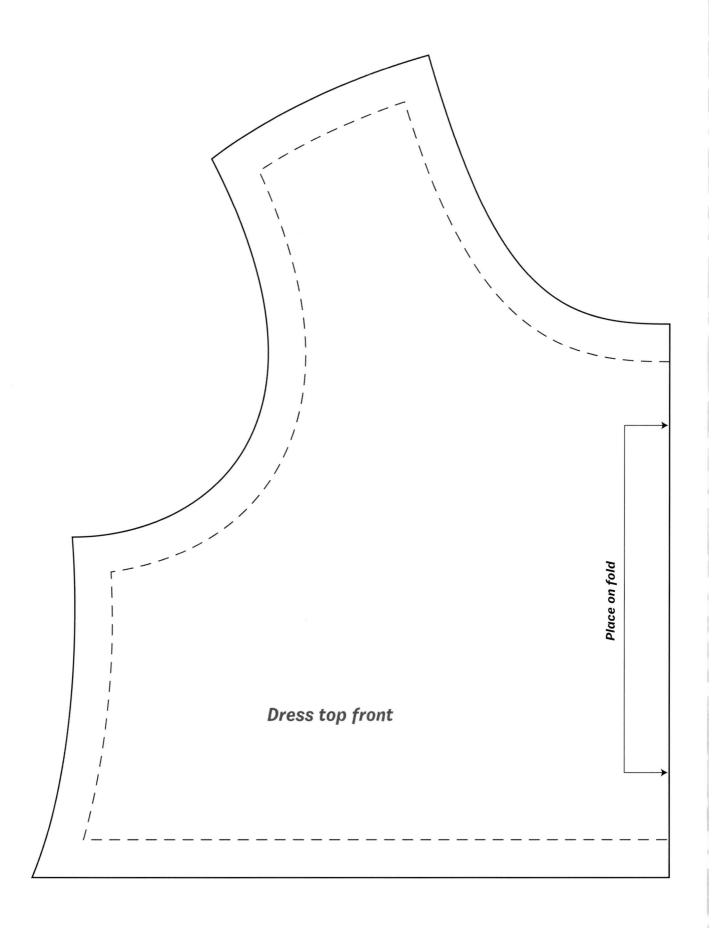

Place on fold

Dress top front

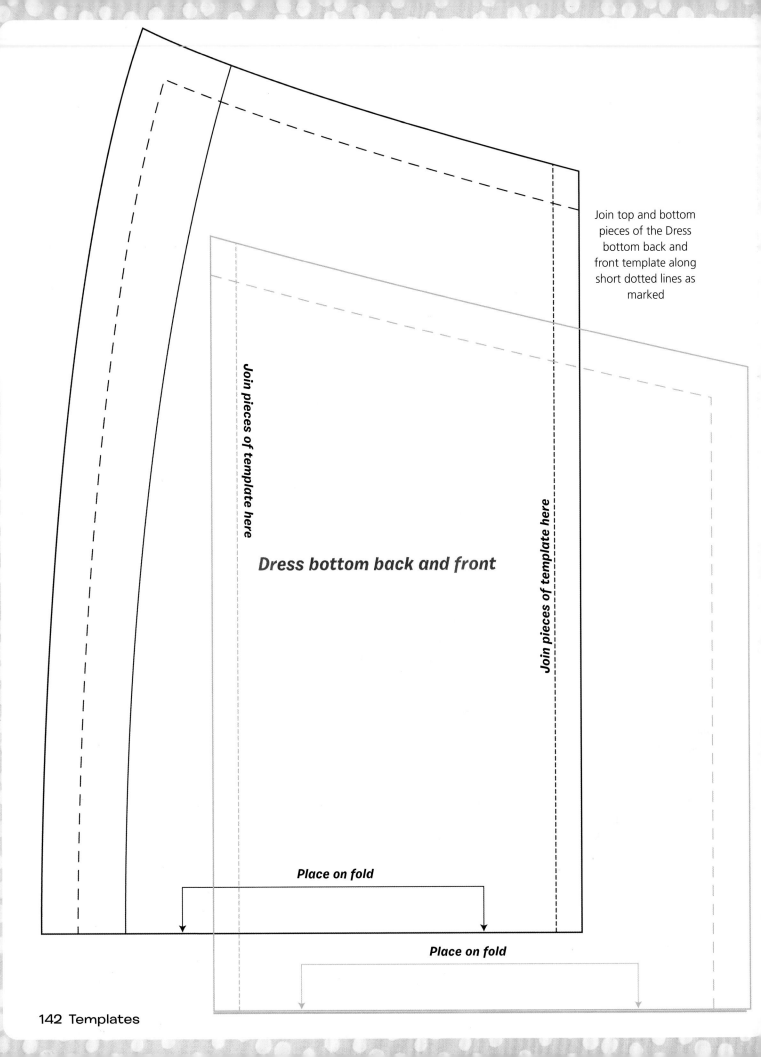

Join top and bottom
pieces of the Dress
bottom back and
front template along
short dotted lines as
marked

Join pieces of template here

Dress bottom back and front

Join pieces of template here

Place on fold

Place on fold

Index

Projects are in **bold**

Acknowledgments

To the wonderful illustrators who were involved: Ingela Aarhenius, Alice Burrows, Gemma Correll, Tom Frost, Nicholas J. Frith, Tove Larris, Luciano Lozano, Sarah McNeil, and Alice Potter—huge, hefty, walloping thanks to all of you. You are amazing. This book wouldn't be what it is without you... so cheers for that!

To Catherine and Charlie, who co-edited the book—humongous gratitude to both of you. Peachy! Thank you.

To my brother, Christian—whopping great thanks for some rather special design work.

To Cindy and everyone at Cico: ta very much for everything—it's been a right royal rollicking laugh.

To my mum—a special thank you! And sorry for the mess... again.

To D-fran—thanks for driving me to shoots, for making everyone lunch and cups of tea, for making me and Claire giggle, especially when you wore the "Beard protector," thanks for everything! You're the bestest x

Illustration credits

Ingela Aarhenius: pp. 24–25, 40–41, 68–71
Alice Burrows: pp. 34–35, 46–49, 86–89, 108–109
Gemma Correll: pp. 18–19, 50–53, 66–67, 90–91, 110–114
Tom Frost: pp. 44–45, 72–73, 92–95
Nicholas J. Frith: front cover, pp. 16–17, 20–23, 32–33, 54–55, 74–79, 106–107
Tove Larris: pp. 98–99, 102–105
Luciano Lozano: pp. 12–15, 42–43, 60–65, 100–101
Sarah McNeil: pp. 8–11, 26–31, 36–39, 56–59, 84–85
Alice Potter: pp. 80–83, 96–97

Template artworks: Stephen Dew